The Land Records

of

Prince George's County
Maryland
1702-1709

Taken from
Microfilm CR 49,514-2

Prince George's County Court Records
Liber C
Archives of Maryland
350 Rowe Boulevard
Annapolis, Maryland 21401

Abstracted by
Elise Greenup Jourdan

HERITAGE BOOKS
2006

HERITAGE BOOKS
AN IMPRINT OF HERITAGE BOOKS, INC.

Books, CDs, and more   Worldwide

For our listing of thousands of titles see our website
at
www.HeritageBooks.com

Published 2006 by
HERITAGE BOOKS, INC.
Publishing Division
65 East Main Street
Westminster, Maryland 21157-5026

International Standard Book Number: 978-1-58549-177-2

FOREWORD

Prince George's County is an old and important county in the development of the Colony of Maryland. In 1696 the upper portions were taken from Calvert and Charles County to form this new county which included all of Western Maryland. By 1748 settlement of the western lands was sufficient to make feasible the formation of Frederick County from portions of Prince George's and Baltimore. In 1776 Montgomery County was cut from the south-eastern portion of Frederick County while Washington County was taken from the north-western part. Washington County was then divided in 1789 to form Allegany County and in 1837 Carroll County was formed from portions of Baltimore and Frederick County. In 1872 the last county to be established in Maryland was taken from the western portion of Allegany and called Garrett County. Thus for 52 years most of the land now belonging to these counties was called Prince George's County. In the 1702-1709 period covered by these records there were few plantations located west of the present-day Montgomery County line, while the area of present-day Prince George's County was so well settled that land was being resurveyed to correct boundaries.

These land records are a valuable resource for genealogists researching Prince George's and surrounding counties. They consist mainly of deeds which show the name of the seller's wife (if any), show her maiden name if the plantation came through her family, and occasionally include the name of the buyer's wife. Sometimes they include the names of children, siblings and other relatives. Many persons from Calvert, Charles, Anne Arundel, Baltimore and St. Mary's Counties bought and sold land recorded in the records during this period as well as Virginians and Englishmen. Merchants and mariners of England and Scotland recorded Letters of Attorney and deeds. There are several leases and deeds of gift of both land and slaves. Oaths of allegiance for the representatives of Queen Ann were recorded.

The spelling of persons, plantations, and landmarks was not consistent, even in the same document. The scribe who wrote the majority of the records consistently spelled field with the letter e before the letter i and his spelling was copied throughout this book. For the most part the spelling is presented in this volume as it appeared on the microfilm, but in some cases it was modernized where it could make no difference to the researcher. Example: Edinburgh instead of Edenborrough. Some of the archaic spelling and peculiar phrasing was included in parenthesis to add interest and color to this book and some was used without parenthesis added. The folio numbering is duplicated in some instances on the original documents, but, since indexing is according to book page number, this should not cause confusion for the researcher.

The English pound sterling was the currency of the Colony. For simplicity this has been presented as £/s/p (pound/shilling/pence) with the numerical figure before the symbol (example: 10£/5s/4p). The survey measurement was a perch which is the equivalent of a present day rod, 5 1/2 yards or 16 1/2 feet. Since both the Julian calendar, which began the new year on March 25th, and the Gregorian calendar, which starts the new year on January 1st, were used, some documents show both dates written, for example, as 1702/3.

In 1699 the Court House and Church Yard were laid out in Charles Towne. In 1707 the first lots were recorded in Charles Towne Court Records for the town of Marlboro. The plat of the Court House and Church Yard of Charles Towne was recorded along with several other plats in the latter part of the Court Records. These interesting drawings have been meticulously copied and included, but it was not possible to copy them to scale working from the microfilm.

It has been my pleasure to abstract this material for publication, and it is my hope that this book will be of value to those interested in the land and the stout-hearted people who settled and developed Prince George's County and the Colony of Maryland.

Elise Greenup Jourdan
Knoxville, Tennessee
Summer 1990

AUGUST COURT 1702
Att a Prince George's County Court held at Charles Town the 24th of August 1702 for our Sovereign
Lady Ann by the Grace of God Queen of England, Scottland, France and Ireland Defender of the
faith and by her Majesties Justices appointed and authorized (VIZ)

| Coll. Thomas Hollyday | John Wight | Robert Bradley | William Hutchison |
| Robert Tyler | Sam'll Magruder | Thomas Sprigg | John Hawkins | Robert Wade |

• *folio 1* • Indenture, 12 Aug 1702
From: **William Skinner,** planter of Calvert County and wife **Elizabeth**
To: **Ignatius Craycroft,** merchant of Prince George's County
    189 acres called *Hatchett* in Prince George's County on the west bank of the Patuxent River
sold for 94£/10s; bounded by *Brooke Creek Manor* and land laid out for **Corneilius Canedy**
Signed: **William Skinner** and **Elizabeth Skinner** (mark)
Witnessed: **Thomas Hollyday, Robert Bradly,** and **Clark Skinner**
Memorandum: 12 Aug 1702 **Elizabeth Skinner,** wife of William, examined by **Thomas Hollyday**
and **Rob't Bradly**
Alienation: 13 Aug 1702 from **Ignatius Craycroft** the sum of 7s/6p
Recorded: 11 Sep 1702

• *folio 2* • Indenture, 15 Feb 1700
From: **Thomas Brooke, Esq'r** of Prince George's County
To: **Joseph Perry,** carpenter of Prince George's County
    173 acres: 109 acre part of *Brookefeild* and 64 acre part of *Addition To Brookefeild* sold for 50£;
lying in Prince George's County
Signed: **Thomas Brooke**
Witnessed: **William Smith** and **William Barton**
Acknowledgement: 20 Feb 1700 **Thomas Brooke** and **Barbara** his wife before **Tho. Greenfeild** and
John Wight
Alienation: **Joseph Perry** the full sums of 4s/10p for the use of **Richard Bennett** and **James Heath**
Recorded: 11 Sep 1702

• *folio 3* • Indenture for 500 years, 25 Aug 1702
From: **William Greenup,** planter of Prince George's County
To: **Thomas Hollyday** of Prince George's County, Gent.
    100 acres of *Cumberland,* part of *Cobreth's Lott* in Prince George's County lying on the east
side of Collington Run on Little Branch for 47£/13s/10p; with 47£/13s/4p due 2 Aug next; to revert to
William Greenup if second payment not made; bounded by *Thorpe Land* or *Beargarden* owned by
John Brown
Signed: **William Greenup**
Witnessed: **Robert Tyler** and **Sam Magruder**
Endorsement on back: **Mary Greenup,** wife of William
Recorded: 12 Sep 1702
(Ed: **William Greenup** purchased this land 27 Oct 1701 from **John Lashley** for 50£; the land
reverted to **Wm. Greenup** after the death of **Thomas Hollyday**; resold 10 Aug 1705 to **Dr. George
Smith** of Baltimore for 95£)

• *folio 5* • Indenture, 10 Jul 1702
From: **Thomas Stone,** planter of Calvert County
To: **Joshua Cecill** of Prince George's County
    200 acre tract called *Margery* in Prince George's County for 20£; lying on the west side of the
Patuxent River bounded by land laid out for **Alexander Magruder;** one-half of this land
bequeathed to **Thomas Stone** by will of **Capt. Richard Gardiner**
Signed: **Thomas Stone** (mark)
Witnessed: **Thos. Hollyday, Robert Bradley,** and **Minanius Bailey** (mark)
Memorandum: 13 Jul 1702

1

Alienation: **Joshua Cecell** paid 8s on 20 Aug 1702
Recorded: 12 Sep 1702
(Ed: Prince George's County Land Records, Vol. I, p. 9: Deed of Gift of 1/2 of *Margery* to **William Wittam** by **Margery Gardiner**, 4 Nov 1696, for "several good causes".)

• *folio 6a* • Indenture, 18 Aug 1702
From: **Thomas Clegett**, Gent. of Calvert County & wife **Sarah**
To: **William Wadsworth**, planter of Calvert County
    250 acres of *Weston* on the west side of the west branch of Patuxent River in Prince George's County for "natural love and affection and for his better support & maintenance"; bounded by *Greenland* laid out for **William Green**, and *Kingston* laid out for **Peter Joy**; on Cabin Branch
Signed: Bottom of page including signature missing
Endorsement: **Sarah Cleggett** examined by **Sam'll Wadsworth**, **John Smith**, and **Thomas Johnson**.
Recorded: 18 Aug 1702
Vide ye alienation in folio 60

• *folio 7* • Indenture, 5 Aug 1702
From: **John Fowler, Sr.**, planter of Prince George's County
To: **David Davis**, planter of Prince George's County
    100 acres called *Fowlers Delight* in Prince George's County in the freshes on west side of Patuxent laid out for **John Fowler** on 13 Aug 1684 for 2,000 pounds of good sound merchantable tobacco; bounded by land taken up by **Major Charles Butler** and by *Beale's Chance*
Signed: **John Fowler**
Memorandum: 25 Aug 1702
Witnessed: **Robert Wade** and **Sam Magruder**
Alienation: From **David Davis** the sum of 4s for use of **Richard Bennett**, **James Heath**, & **William Barton**
Recorded: 14 Sep 1702

• *folio 8* • Indenture, 10 Jul 1702
From: **Roger Brooke**, Gent. of Calvert County
To: **Thomas Blandford**, planter of Prince George's County
    Timberland, 154 acres in Prince George's County for 50£; bounded by *Brooke Wood* owned by **Robert Brooke** and land sold by **Thomas Brooke** to **Thomas Bratt**
Signed: **Roger Brooke** (mark)
Witnessed: **Tho. Taney, Clarke Skinner, Martha_____**
Memorandum: witnessed by **Thos. Greenfeild** and **Just Provin**
Alienation: 23 Feb 1702 **Thos. Blandford** paid the sum of 6s
Recorded: 1 Sep 1702

• *folio 9* • Indenture, 12 Aug 1702
From: **Thomas James**, planter of Prince George's County
To: **Edward Willett** of Prince George's County
    103 acres on Beaver Dam Branch called *Little Deare* formerly in Calvert Co., now in Prince George's County for 3,000 pounds of good merchantable tobacco; land surveyed by **Daniel Elliott**; bounded by Beaver Dam Run; Royal mines excepted
Signed: **Thomas James** (mark)
Witnessed: **Thomas Hollyday** and **James Stoddart**
Memorandum: Endorsement on back of **Elizabeth**, wife of **Thomas James**; witnessed by **Thomas Hollyday** and **James Stoddart**.
Alienation: 23 Feb 1702/3 **Edward Willett** paid the sum of 4s
Vide ye alienation in folio 43

• *folio 10* • Public Instrument, relating to estate of **Richard Allen**, dec'd, haberdasher of London; will probated in Canterbury, England, in the time of Lord William, King of England

2

From: **Joseph Webb**, grocer of London and his wife **Sarah**, daughter of **Richard Allen**, heirs of the Maryland estate of **Richard Allen**
Letter of Attorney: To **John Parker**, merchant of London traveling to Maryland, to collect debt due Allen estate from **Edward Willett**, late of London, now of Maryland
Signed: **Joseph Webb** and **Sarah Webb**
Witnessed: **Philip James, Sam'll Bourns,** and **W. Botteler,** filed and duly stamped
Probate document written in Latin, filed "Londini septieno die Augusti 1700"; **Tho. Wellham,** Reg'ty Dep'tus; signed **Guil Scarey,** Nonair Publicus

• *folio 11* • Instrument of Procuration, 7 Aug 1700
From: **John Parker,** formerly of London, presently residing Philadelphia, Pennsylvania
To: **Jacob Regnier** of Annapolis, to act as agent in the matter of the heirs **Joseph Webb** and his wife **Sarah** to the estate of **Richard Allen,** dec'd, haberdasher of London
Signed: **John Parker** 18 Apr 1702
Witnessed: **Henry Grubb, Isaac Meriatt,** and **Henry Collingson**

• *folio 11a* • From **John Parker** to **Edward Willett**; notification of substitution of **Jacob Regnier** to handle affairs of estate of **Richard Allen**
Signed: **John Parker,** 6 Jul 1702

• *folio 11a* • Indenture, 19 Aug 1702
From: **Edward Willett,** pewterer of Prince George's County and wife **Tabitha**
To: **Jacob Regnier, Esq'r,** of Lincolns Inn Middlesex, England, now living in Maryland
   For 250£ the 157 acres in Prince George's County called *The Horserace* containing 300 acres formerly located in Calvert County; sold by **James Moor** to **Edward Willett**; the other part purchased by **Thomas Cox**; and for 173£/10s another parcel of land called *Little Deare* containing 103 acres formerly taken up by **Thomas James** said to be in Charles County but was also in Prince George's County; five payments to be made at Annapolis at the State House
Signed: **Ja. Regnier**
Witnessed: **Rich'd Pile** and **Hen. Collingson**

• *folio 13* • Obligation, 19 Aug 1702
From: **Jacob Regnier** of Lincolns Inn, Middlesex, England, now living in Maryland
To: **Edward Willett,** pewterer of Prince Georges Co., and wife; 346£
Signed: **Jacob Regnier** on 19 Aug 1702
Witnessed: **Rich'd Pile** and **Hen. Collingson**

SEPTEMBER COURT 1702
(top part of page missing)

Coll. Thomas Hollyday	John Wight	Robert Bradley	William Hutchison			
Robert Tyler	Sam'll Magruder	Thomas Sprigg	John Hawkins	Robert Wade	James Stoddart	

• *folio 13a* • Indenture, 26 Jun 1702
From: **Nathan Veitch,** planter of Prince George's County and his wife **Anne Veitch**
To: **Hon. Col. Henry Darnall,** Gent. of Prince George's County
   For 50£ a 125 acre part of the *Expedition of Beall,* formerly of Calvert County, now lying in Prince George's County on the west side of the Patuxent River; bounded by Cabin Branch
Signed: **Nathan Veitch** and **Anne Veitch**
Witnessed: **Sam'll Magruder** and **James Stoddart**
Endorsement on back: 28 Sep 1702 **Anne Veitch** examined by **Sam'll Magruder** and **James Stoddart**

• *folio 14a* • Indenture, 12 Aug 1702
From: **William Skinner,** planter of Calvert County
To: **Clarke Skinner,** planter of Calvert County

The Lord Baron of Baltimore did grant at St. Mary's on 23 Jun 1680 to **James Nuthall** 300 acres in the woods on the west side of the Patuxent River called *Hatchett;* **James Nuthall** and his wife **Margaret** sold the land to **Robert Skinner** 8 Mar 1686; **Robert Skinner** gave the land to his 3rd son **William Skinner** and he sold 111 acres of the land to his brother, **Clarke Skinner,** for an uspecified amount of money; bounded by land **Cornelius Cannaday** sold **Ignatius Craycroft** Endorsement on back: **Elizabeth Skinner** examined by **Thom. Hollyday** and **Rob't Bradley** Witnessed: **Thom. Hollyday, Rob't Bradley,** and **Igna. Craycroft** Vide ye alienation in folio 43

• *folio 15a* • Indenture, 17 Oct 1701
From: **George Plowden,** Gent. of St. Mary's County
To: **Maj. Wm. Barton,** Gent. of Prince George's County
 For 35,000 pounds of good merchantable tobacco sold 800 acres of land called *Perrywood* formerly in Calvert County now Prince George's County; bounded by the main branch of the dividing creek of the Patuxent River and land patented on 10 Jun 1671 to **Richard Perry** Signed: **George Plowden**
Acknowledged: **Tho. Brooke** and **John Wight**
Witnessed: **Vincent Lambert** and **Henry Bonner**
Alienation: 27 Aug 1702 by **Maj. Wm. Barton**

• *folio 16a* • Indenture, 3 Oct 1701
From: **Nicholas & Rob't Brent,** Gent. of the Colony of Virginia; execx. of last will of **George Brent**
To: **Major Wm. Barton** of Prince George's County
 200 acres called *Willard's Purchase* on west side of Patuxent adjacent to **James Godgrace** property and next to land granted **Thomas Hatton,** sold by him to **Hugh Stanley,** uncle of **John Stanley;** and 400 acres of a neck of land lying between Swanson's alias Freshams Creek and the Patuxent River near *Willard's Purchase* "**John Stanley,** called **John Stanley** of Calvert County, Mariner, joint tenants in common with his brother **Edward Stanley**" sold on 15 Oct 1690 to **Henry Brent,** Gent. of Calvert County, 2 parcels of land, one called *Willard's Purchase* originally recorded in records of Calvert County
Signed: **Nicho. Brent** and **Rob't Brent**
Witnessed: **Robert Bradley** and **James Stoddart**
Alienation: 10 Oct 1701 the sum of 6s paid by **Maj. William Barton**
 Maj. Barton required adding to the record a codicil of **George Brent** written 28 Mar 1698 requiring the Maryland land be sold which mentions his brother **Henry Brent** and my heirs **Henry, Mary** and **Martha Brent;** land called *Pitchcroft* of 400 acres, land at Swanson's Creek in Patuxent of 300 acres, *Rich Leavell* in Baltimore County of 600 acres, and "*Pokemoke,* my part of 1300 acres"

• *folio 18* • Indenture, 4 Jul 1702
From: **Joshua Cecell** of Prince George's County and wife **Mary Cecell**
To: **John Deakins,** carpenter of Prince George's County
 100 acres of *Mount Calvert Manor* excepting 4 acres belonging to **John Davis,** formerly owned by **Wm. Stone** and **John Meriton** and 2 acres formerly leased to **Joshua Cecell** who purchased this land from **John Davis** and wife **Elizabeth** of Prince George's Co., 27 Sep 1698; located in the freshes near the dividing creek of the Patuxent River
Signed: **Joshua Cecell**
Witnessed: **Thomas Hollyday** and **John Senman**
Memorandum: Examination of **Mary Cecill,** wife of Joshua on 26 Nov 1702
Acknowledged in open court

• *folio 20* • Indenture, 5 Aug 1702
From: **Ninean Beall,** Gent. of Prince George's County and wife **Ruth**
To: **Wm. Offett,** planter of Prince George's County
 The Gleaning in consideration of land taken away by an older survey; 77 acres in Prince George's County on the west side of the Patuxent bounded by land of **John Darnall** Signed: **Ninean Beall**

4

Acknowledged: **Ruth Beall** signed 25 Aug 1702; witnessed by **Robert Tyler** and **Robert Wade**
Recorded: Alienation of **Wm. Offett** 25 Nov 1702

• *folio 22* • Indenture, 4 Jun 1701
From: **Col. Ninian Beall** of Prince George's County, Gent.
To: **William Offett**, planter of Prince George's County
    Darnall's Good Will of 450 acres for 120£; bounded by *Darnall's Good Luck*, land already belonging to **Wm. Offett**, and a tract belonging to **Mr. Charles Carroll**
Signed: **Ninean Beall**
Witnessed: **John Murdock** and **John Holdiworth**
Acknowledged: 26 Aug 1701 **Ruth Beall** signed; witnessed by **Rob't Tyler** and **Tho. Sprigg**

• *folio 25* • Condition of Obligation, 13 Oct 1702
From: **Edward Willett** and **Thomas Box**
To: **Thomas Dent** of Prince George's County
    Thomas Dent, appointed the lawful Clerk of Prince George's County and **Edward Willett** appointed his Deputy Clerk
Signed: **Edward Willet** and **Thomas Box**
Witnessed: **Tabitha Willet** (mark) and **Caleb Norris** (mark)
Alienation: 22 Dec 1698 **Thomas Wells** (sic) the sum of 8s for 200 acres
Vide ye convenyance in Liber A., folio 26

• *folio 26* • 9 Sep 1702
From: **Thomas Dent**
To: **Edward Willett**
    "By virtue of the power and authority to me granted by The Honorable **Sir Thomas Lawrence**, Baronet, Secretary of Maryland to be keeper of the records and clerk of Prince George's County Court" **Edward Willett** is appointed Deputy Clerk and allowed to keep 1/2 of the fees collected.

JANUARY COURT 1702

Att a Prince George's County Court held at Charles Town the 26th of January 1702 for our Sovereign Lady Ann by the Grace of God Queen of England, Scotland, France and Ireland Defender of the faith and by her Majesties Justices appointed and authorized (VIZ)

William Hutchison	John Wight	Robert Bradley	Robert Tyler	William Tannyhill
John Hawkins	Robert Wade	Samuell Magruder	Thomas Sprigg	James Stoddart

---

• *folio 26* • Indenture, 25 May 1701
From: **Joseph Duglace** of Charles County, Gent.
To: **Francis Collier** of Calvert County
    For 50£ a 100 acre parcel of the 1,050 acre *Coole Spring Manner* in Fendall's fresh; originally granted to **Capt. Josias Fendall** now occupied by Duglace
Signed: **Joseph Duglace**
Witnessed: **William Hollyday** and **Joshua Hall**
Endorsement: 28 May 1701 signed **Rob't Tyler** and **James Stoddart**
Alienation: 25 Jun 1701 **Francis Collier** paid the sum of 2s, 100 acres of land for use of **Rich'd Bennett** and **James Heath**

• *folio 27* • Indenture, 8 Oct 1698
From: **Francis Collier** of Prince George's County, Gent.
To: **Guy White**, carpenter of Prince George's County
    50 acres part of *Cold Spring Manor* on the west side of the Patuxent River in Prince George's County to a branch by the mouth of Stafford's Cove for 5,000 pounds of tobacco
Signed: **Francis Collier**
Witnessed: **Hugh Riley** and **John Browne**
Endorsed: **Sarah**, wife of **Francis Collier**; witnessed by **Robert Tyler** and **Samuell Magruder**
Alienation: 15 Nov 1698 the sum of 1s paid by **Guy White**

5

• *folio 30* • Obligation, 8 Oct 1698
From: **Francis Collier** of Prince George's County, Gent.
To: **Guy White**, carpenter of Prince George's County
  Francis Collier binds himself to pay **Guy White** 8,000 pounds of tobacco "according to Act of the Assembly"
Signed: **Francis Collier**
Witnessed: **Rob't Tyler** and **Samuel Magruder**

• *folio 31* • Indenture, 7 May 1701
From: **Joseph Duglace**, Gent. of Charles County
To: **Guy White**
  For 185£ a parcel of 100 acres of the 1050 acre *Coole Spring Manor* granted **Capt. Josiah Fendall** bounded by a run called Bower Brook and land of **Mr. Francis Collier**
Signed: **Joseph Duglace**
Witnessed: **William Hollyday** and **Joshua Hall**
Endorsement: 28 May 1701 signed by **Robt. Tyler** and **James Stoddart**
Alienation: 25 Jun 1701 for the sum of 17s/6p paid by **Guy White**

• *folio 32* • Indenture, 12 Feb 1701
From: **Wallter Hope** of Blandford Farm in the County of Dorsett
To: **Wm. Hutchison** of Prince George's County
  For 40£ two tracts of land totalling 660 acres; one tract called *Happy* on the north side of the Eastern Branch of the Potomac River bounded by land laid out for **Walter Thompson**; the second tract called *Hope's Addition* lying between *Happy* and a tract called *Turkey Busard* owned by **Collonell Rosiar**
Signed: **Wallter Hope**
Witnessed: **Robt. Tyler**, Mayor of Corbin, **Thomas Caywell**, and **Jos. Thompson**
Endorsement: 2 Jan 1702
Alienation: The sum of 26 shillings from Mr. **James Stoddart** for 2 tracts of land
Above deed acknowledged by Mr. **James Stoddart** by virtue of letter of attorney recorded in folio 139

• *folio 33* • Indenture, 9 Jan 1702
From: **Samuel Taylor** of Prince George's County, Gent.
To: **Samuell, Joseph,** and **Hannah Copeland**, only children of the late **Sam'll Copeland** of Prince George's County
  For a valuable consideration 50 acres of land in the freshes of the Patuxent River on the south side of **Samuel Taylor's** land; in Deep Spring Branch; adjoining *Coxe's Hayes* near **Peter Archer's** orchard to corner of land sold this day to **Thomas Loyd** by **Samuell Taylor**
Signed: **Samuel Taylor**
Endorsement: 9 Jan 1702 by **Verlinda Taylor**, wife of Samuel
Acknowledged and Witnessed: **Tho. Greenfeild** and **John Wight**
Alienation: 26 Jan 1702 received of **Thomas Loyd** the sum of 1s

• *folio 35* • Indenture, 9 Jan 1702
From: **Samuel Taylor**, Gent. of Prince George's County
To: **Thomas Loyde**, planter of Prince George's County
  52 acres for 43£/10s in the freshes of the Patuxent River
Signed: **Samuel Taylor**
Witnessed: **Thomas Greenfeild** and **John Wight**
Endorsement: 9 Jan 1702 **Verlinda Taylor**; acknowledged by **Thomas Greenfeild** and **John Wight**
Alienation: 26 Jan 1702 Rec'd of **Thomas Loyd** the sum of 1s

• *folio 37* • Indenture 26 Jan 1702/3
From: **Col. Ninian Beall** formerly of Calvert County, now of Prince George's & wife **Ruth Beall**
To: **James Butler** formerly of Calvert County, now of Prince George's
  One acre of land for 15s from the 82 acres of a warrant of 3,000 acres due **Ninian Beall** dated 1 Apr 1684 lying on the west side of Western Branch in the woods called *The Meadows* bounded by

6

land surveyed for **Thomas Brooke** called *Greene's Landing*, land of **John Bigger**, and land called *Bacon's Hall*; certificate of survey at land office at St. Mary's 15 Sep 1694
Signed: **Ninian Beall** and **Ruth Beall**
Witnessed: **Wm. Tannyhill** and **Samuel Magruder**
Endorsement: 6 Jan 1702/3 **Ruth Beall** examined by same
Alienation: 27 Jan 1702/3 the sum of one half-penny rec'd of **James Butler**

* *folio 38* • Indenture, 16 Jan 1702
From: **John Tato**, planter of Prince George's County
To: **John Mills**, planter of Prince George's County
  For 30£ and 3,100 pounds of good merchantable tobacco for 100 acre tract; bounded by land laid out for **John Pott** called *Mount Pleasant* and the Patuxent River
Signed: **John Tato** (mark)
Endorsement: **William Lee** and **Joshua Hall**
Acknowledged: 16 Jan 1702/3 by **R. Bradly** and **James Stoddart**
Alienation: 26 Jan 1702 received of **John Mills** the sum of 2s

* *folio 39* • Obligation, 16 Jan 1702
From: **John Tato**, Planter of Prince George's County
To: **John Mills**, planter of Prince George's County
  John Tato agrees to pay **John Mills** 60£ and 6,200 of good merchantable tobacco
Signed: **John Tato** (mark)
Witnessed: **William Lee** and **Joshua Hall**

* *folio 39* • Indenture, no date
From: **Samuel Taylor** and **Verlinda Taylor** of Prince George's County
To: **Mr. William Hutchison** and his wife **Sarah** of Prince George's County
  Satarday's Work of 500 acres formerly in Charles County; for a "certain indenture or bargaine & sale....for halfe of a certaine parcell of land given **Verlinda Taylor** by the will of her late father **Robert Doyne**"; bounded by Run of Kiskonken Creek, a tide run, and *Zechia Manor*
Signed: **Sam'll Taylor** and **Verlinda Taylor**
Witnessed: **Thos. Greenfeild**
Memorandum: **Verlinda Taylor** examined 9 Jan 1702/3 by **Tho. Greenfeild** and **John Wight**

* *folio 39a* • Indenture, 14 Jan 1702
From: **Thomas Greenfeild** of Prince George's County, Gent.
To: **Nicholas Davis**, planter of Prince George's County
  For 6,000 pounds of good tobacco for 2 parcels of land, one called *Quick Sale* containing 60 acres in the freshes of the Patuxent River; bounded by land of **Samuel Taylor**, **Wm. Bayley**, and land called *Newton;* another parcel of a 50 acre part of *Archers Pasture*
Signed: **Tho. Greenfeild**
Witnessed: **Tho. Brooke** and **Ninian Beall**
Memorandum: **Martha**, wife of **Thomas Greenfeild**, examined by **Wm. Barton** and **John Wight**
Alienation: 23 Feb 1702/3 the sum of 3s/2 1/2p paid by **Nicholas Davis**

* *folio 40a* • Indenture, 25 Mar 1702
From: **Robert Tyler** of Prince George's County, Gent.
To: **Abraham Clarke** of Prince George's County, Gent.
  For 160£ a 400 acre tract of *Darnalls Grove* called *Clarke's Forest* in the freshes of the Patuxent River; bounded by Collington Branch, *His Lordship's Manor,* a tract of land laid out for **Lewis Devall**, and in a line of **Samuell Devall**; Royal mines excepted
Signed: **Robert Tyler**
Witnessed: **William Slone** and **Richard Gambra**
Endorsement: **Susanah Tyler** 25 Mar 1702
Alienation: 25 Jan 1702 **Abraham Clarke** paid the sum of 16s

- *folio 41a* • Indenture, 9 Jan 1702
From: **Samuel Taylor**, planter of Prince George's County
To: **Hezekiah Bussee/Bussey**, planter of Prince George's County
50£ to be paid to **Thomas Smith** of Calvert County for land called *Taylor's Marsh* and that part of another parcel of land laid out for 600 acres lying together in the freshes of the Patuxent River; bounded by land formerly belonging to **Peter Archer**, dec'd, Taylor's Creek, and through a marsh to the river
Signed: **Samuel Taylor**
Witnessed: **Tho. Greenfeild** and **John Wightt**
Memorandum: **Verlinda**, wife of **Samuel Taylor** signed endorsement 9 Jan 1702; witnessed by same
Alienation: 23 Feb 1702/3 **Hezekiah Buissey** paid the sum of 2s

- *folio 43* • Vide conveyance in folio 14, this record: 23 Feb 1702/3 **Clarke Skinner**
- *folio 43* • Vide conveyance in Liber A, folio 437: 23 Feb 1702/3 **Edward Willett**
- *folio 43* • Vide conveyance in folio 9, this record: 23 Feb 1702/3 **Edward Willett**

- *folio 43* • Condition of Obligation, 12 Jan 1702
From: **Henry Acton**
To: **Coll. Ninian Beall** and **Thomas Dickeson**
Regarding the sale of the estate of **Richard Gambra**
Signed: **Hen. Acton**
Witnessed: **Edward Willett** and **John Barker**

- *folio 43a* • Discharge of Obligation, Maryland, 9 Jul 1701
From: **Benjamin Hadduck**
To: **Coll'll Ninian Beall**
"Bee it knowne unto all men that I, **Benjamin Hadduck** doe quitt and discharge **Coll. Ninian Beall** of all accomph bills bonds and all other things whatsoever from ye beginning of ye world to ye day of the date here of WITNESSETH hereof I have hereunto putt my hand and seale"
The marks of   **Benjamin Hadduck** (seal)
Simon Nickholl
John Holdsworth

- *folio 43a* • Indenture, 25 Aug 1702
From: **Ninian Beale** of Prince George's County, Gent.
To: **James Beale**, planter of Prince George's County
111£ for 550 acres in 2 tracts of land; 466 acres called *Rover's Content* bounded by land of **Wallter Evans**, *His Lordship's Manor*, and **Mr. Carroll's** land; and an 89 acre part of a tract called *The Enclosure*
Signed: **Ninean Beall**
Memorandum: Endorsement of **Ruth Beall**, wife of Ninian
Witnessed: **Rob't Tyler** and **Rob't Wade**
Alienation: 26 Nov 1702; **Henry Darnall** shows receipt bearing date 11 Feb 1698 with mistake in conveyance; above deed confirmed

---

MARCH COURT 1702/3
Att a Prince George's County Court held at Charles Towne the 23rd day of March 1702/3 for our Sovereign Lady Ann by the Grace of God of England, Scottland, France and Ireland Queen Defender of the Faith by her Majesties Justices thereunto authorized, VIZ
William Hutchison   John Wight   Robert Bradly   Robert Tyler   William Tannyhill
John Hawkins   Robert Wade   Samuell Magruder   Thomas Sprigg   James Stoddart

---

- *folio 44a* • Indenture, 8 Mar 1702
From: **Robert Tyler** of Prince George's County, Gent.
To: **Col. Henry Ridgly**, merchant of Prince George's County

200£ for 500 acres of *Marye's Delight* from a tract called *Darnall's Grove;* bounded by land laid out for **Richard Robson** and *Darnall's Grove;* Royal mines excepted
Signed: **Rob't Tyler**
Memorandum: 8 Mar 1702 **Susannah Tyler** examined by **Samuell Magruder** & **Tho's Sprigg, Jr.**
Witnessed: **Thomas Odell, Richard Duckett**
Alienation: **Major Barton** paid 24 Sep 1700 for this land; not recorded; cancelled deed shown

- *folio 45a* • Indenture, 8 Mar 1702
From: **Henry Ridgley**, merchant, and **Rob't Tyler, Gent.**, both of Prince George's County
To: **Lewis Devall**, planter of Anne Arundel County
    24£/4s for a 63 acre tract of land called *Devall's Cowpen,* part of a tract called *Ridgley's and Taylor's Chance* bounded by *Willson's Plaines* now in the possession of **Mareen Devall, Jr.**; Royal mines excepted
Signed: **Henry Ridgly** (mark) and **Rob't Tyler**
Memorandum: Endorsement on back of **Mary Ridgley** and **Susanna Tyler**; signed **Samuell Magruder** and **Tho. Sprigg, Jr.**
Witnessed: **Samuel Magruder** and **Rich'd Duckett**
Alienation: 23 Mar 1702/3 the sum of 2s from **Lewis Devall**

- *folio 46a* • Indenture, 8 Mar 1702
From: **Col. Henry Ridgley**, merchant, and **Robert Tyler, Gent.**, both of Prince George's County
To: **Thomas Fowler**, planter of Prince George's County
    For 20£ a tract of 100 acres called *Fowler's Venture* being part of *Ridgleys and Taylor's Chance;* bounded by a parcel of land laid out for **John Howerton** called *Howerton's Range* now in the possession of **William Orrick** and **Benjamin Duvall**; Royal mines excepted
Signed: **Henry Ridgley** (mark) and **Robert Tyler**
Memorandum: On the back of the deed 8 Mar 1702 signed by **Mary Ridgley** and **Susanna Tyler**; examined by **Sam'll Magruder** and **Thomas Sprigg, Jr.**
Witnessed: **Samuell Magruder** and **Richard Duckett**
Alienation: 23 Mar 1702/3 from **Thomas Fowler** the sum of 4s

- *folio 48* • Indenture, 8 Mar 1702
From: **Coll. Henry Ridgley**, merchant, and **Robert Tyler, Gent.**, both of Prince George's County
To: **Thomas Ricketts**, planter of Anne Arundel County
    For 120£ a tract of land containing 300 acres, being part of *Ridgley and Taylor's Chance* lying in Prince George's County; bounded by *Willson's Plaine* now in the possession of **Mareen Duvall, Jr.**, a tract laid out for **Lewis Duvall** which also is part of the land called *Ridgley and Taylor's Chance* (the whole containing 463 acres); also bounding **Thomas Fowler**'s land; Royal mines excepted
Signed: **Henry Ridgley** (mark) and **Robert Tyler**
Memorandum: On the back of the deed the endorsement of **Mary Ridgley** and **Susannah Tyler**, examined by **Sam'll Magruder** and **Tho. Sprigg, Junior**
Witnessed: **Samuell Magruder** and **Rich'd Duckett**
Alienation: 23 Mar 1702 received of **Thomas Rickett** the sum of 12s

- *folio 49a* • Indenture, 8 Mar 1702
From: **Richard Cheyney**, Senior, planter of Anne Arundel County
To: **Charles Cheyney** of Anne Arundel County
    50 acres of land called *Cheyney's Beginning* part of a tract called *Cheyney's Adventures* for diverse and good causes and valuable considerations; lying in Prince George's County on the river and running along a tidal branch; Royal mines excepted
Signed: **Richard Cheyney, Sen'r** (mark)
Witnessed: **Rich'd Duckett** and **Thomas Odell**
Memorandum: 8 Mar 1702 **Mary Chesney**, wife of Richard, examined by **Samuell Magruder** and **Tho. Sprigg, Jnr.**
Alienation: Received from **Robert Tyler** for **Charles Cheyney** the sum of 2s

- *folio 50a* • Indenture, 13 May 1702/3
From: **Notley Roziar** of Port Tobacco in Charles County, Gent.
To: **Thomas Hotchhill**, planter of Prince George's County
  "For and in consideration of the rents and covenants on the tenants or lessees part to be paid performed and fulfilled and other considerations...all the moiety or half part of a tract of land" formerly in Charles County, now in Prince George's County called *St. Elisabeth* on the east side of Piscattaway River in the end of a bay of said river called Thomas Bay; bounded by St. Joseph's Creek
Signed: **Notley Roziar**
Witnessed: **Thomas Hinctt, Phillip Reiley**, and **Nicholas Crouch**

- *folio 51* • Indenture, 24 Apr 1703
From: **James Moor** of Prince George's County
To: **Coll. Henry Darnall** of Prince George's County, Gent.
  For 6,000 pounds of tobacco a parcel of land of 150 acres called *Defence* lying in Calvert County; bounded by land called *Greenland,* a parcel called *Charles Hills*, a branch called Charles Branch and a parcel of land laid out for **William Hale**
Signed: **James Moor**
Witnessed: **Edward Willett** and **David Small**
Memorandum: Endorsement on back 24 Apr 1703 acknowledged by **James Moor** and **Mary**, his wife before **Rob't Tyler** and **Tho's Sprigg, Jun'r**

- *folio 52* • Indenture, 27 Mar 1703
From: **Coll. Henry Darnall** of Prince George's County, Gent.
To: **Phillip Gittings** of Prince George's County, Gent.
  For a tract of land lying in *St. Cullbert Manner* in St. Mary's County called *Grayden* Col. Darnall sells to **Phillip Gittings** a parcel of land containing 269 acres now in the possession of Gittings called *Graiden* lying in Prince Georges County; bounded by a tract of land belonging to **Thomas Lucas**, running to line of **Mr. Thomas Sprigg**
Signed: **Henry Darnall**
Witnessed: **R. Bradly** and **James Stoddart**
Memorandum: Endorsement on back 27 Mar 1703 by **Henry Darnall**; signed by **R. Bradly** and **James Stoddart**
Alienation: 24 May 1703 **Phillip Gettings** paid the sum of 11s

- *folio 53* • Indenture, 24 May 1703
From: **William Hutchison** of Prince George's County, Gent.
To: **John Smith**, planter of Prince George's County
  For 100£ all 654 acres of that parcel of land called *Houp Yard* and all the parcel called *Houp's Addition* containing "the meets and bounds" of both parcels lying in Prince George's County on the north side of the Eastern Branch of the Potomac River; bounded by land of **Wallter Thompson**, land called *Duddington Manner* belonging to **Mr. Roziar**; Royal mines excepted
Signed: **Wm. Hutchison**
Witnessed: **R. Bradly** and **James Stoddart**
Memorandum: 24 May 1703 endorsement on back of deed of **Sarah Hutchison**, wife of William; examined by **R. Bradly** and **James Stoddart**
Alienation: 29 May 1703 **John Smith** paid the sum of 1£/6s

- *folio 54* • Indenture, 20 Apr 1701
From: **Charles** and **Deborah Ridgley** of Prince George's County
To: **Francis Piles**, planter of Prince George's County
  111 acres now farmed by Ridgley from a 1,100 acre tract of land called *Croome* lying in Prince George's County for 53£
Signed: **Charles Ridgley** and **Deborah Ridgley** (her mark)
Memorandum: 26 Nov 1702 endorsement on back of **Deborah Ridgley**, wife of Charles
Witness: **John Hawkins** and **Robert Wade**
Alienation: 23 Jan rec'd of **Francis Piles** the sum of 3s

- *folio 55* • Indenture, 13 Jul 1701
From: **Coll. Henry Darnall**, agent for The Right Honorable Charles, Lord Barron of Baltimore
To: **Jonathan Simons**, tailor of Prince George's County
    By document dated London, 28 Nov 1691, Col. Darnall was authorized to act in the manner he "shall think fit" regarding distribution of His Lordship's land in Prince George's County. This tract of land containing 200 acres lying in the *Westerne Branch Manner;* bounded by **Thomas Spriggs;** for the natural life of **Jonathan Simons**, his wife **Elizabeth,** and his son **Joseph Simons** for payment of 4£ and annual rent of 20s and 2 capons to be paid at the feast of the Nativity; they shall plant 400 apple trees and maintain the orchard; at the end of the 3 lives the fences and enclosures shall be in repair and the land revert to the heirs of Lord Baltimore
Signed: **Henry Darnall**
Witnessed: **Clement Hill, Jr.** and **Henry Darnall, Jr.**

- *folio 55a* • Indenture, 13 June 1701
From: **Coll. Henry Darnall**, agent for **The Right Honorable Charles, Lord Barron of Baltimore**
To: **Joseph Browne**, planter of Prince George's County
    By document dated London, 28 Nov 1691, Col. Darnall was authorized to act in the manner he "shall think fit" regarding distribution of His Lordship's land in Prince George's County. This tract of land containing 200 acres lying in the *Western Branch Manner;* bounded by land of **Charles Wallker** and **James Mullikan;** for the natural life of **Joseph Browne**, his wife **Ann Browne** and their daughter **Sarah Browne** for payment of 4£ and an annual rent of 20s and 2 capons to be paid at the feast of the Nativity; they shall plant 400 apple trees and maintain the orchard; at the end of the 3 lives the fences and enclosure shall be in repair and the land revert to the heirs of Lord Baltimore
Signed: **Henry Darnall**
Witnessed: **Clement Hill, Jr.** and **Henry Darnall, Jr.**

- *folio 56a* • Publick Instrument of Procuration, 1 Feb 1692
From: **Peter Pagon**, merchant of London
To: **Isaack Millner**, merchant of London
    Letter of Attorney: Before **Porton Paul**, Public Notary of London, **Peter Pagon** appoints **Isaac Millner** of London, a merchant bound for the Province of Maryland, to be his attorney with full power to demand payment of sums of money, tobacco, goods, effects and things whatsoever which any person or persons is of are owing or indebted to him and to appoint one or more attorneys in Maryland to act for him.
Signed: **Peter Pagon**
Witness: **John Harwood**
Certified: **P. Paul**

- *folio 57* • Power of Attorney, 13 Mar 1697
From: **Isaac Millner**, Factor to **Peter Paggon** and Company of London, merchants
To: **John Ferry**, and others
    Letter of Attorney: Mr. Millner assigned his power to act for **Peter Paggon** and Company to the following: "My trusty and well beloved friends" **John Ferry** of Baltimore County, Gentleman, **Edward Stevenson** of Patapsco River, **Samuell Sicklemoor** of Gunpowder River in said county and **John Garrard** of South River in Anne Arundell County, merchants. These men empowered to act for both Millner and Paggon.
Signed: **Isaac Millner**
Witnessed: **John Hayes, Will'm Willkeson** (mark), and **Tobiah Schamburgh** (mark)

- *folio 57* • Power of Attorney, 16 Mar in the first year of the reign of Queen Anne
From: **Samuel Bigg** of Prince George's County
To: **John Lambe** of Anne Arundel County
    Samuel Bigg states that in his absence **John Lamb** is appointed to act as his attorney with full power to carry on his business affairs.
Signed: **Sam'll Bigg**
Witnessed: **William Nicholson** and **Francis Colliar**

- *folio 57a* • Action of Debt, 26 Apr ____
From: **Mr. Wm. Round** and Company
Against: **Kathrine Willson & Josh Cecell**
   "The Plantives sued ye defendants in an action of debt for 15£ and recovered judgement against ye said defendants for the said debt together with pounds of tobacco cost of suit. and now here at this day that is to say ye 26th day of April came Mr. **James Stoddart** attorney or factor of ye said **James Rounds and Company** and acknowledgeth that he is sattidfyed with debt and damages afforesaid. Therefore lett ye said **Kathrine Willson** and **Joshua Cecill** of ye debt and damages aforesaid be acquitted."

- *folio 57a* • Indenture, 23 Mar 1703
From: **Andrew Hambleton**, planter of Prince George's County, and uxor
To: **William Tanyhill**, planter of Prince George's County
   16£ paid for part of a tract called *Attwood's Purchase* lying in Prince George's County on the south side of the Eastern Branch of the Potomac River of 122 acres; bounded by *Akin Head* owned by **William Tannyhill**, running with the channel of Pasture Branch
Signed: **Andrew Hambleton** and **Mary Hambleton**
Witnessed: **Fra. Wheeler** and **Thomas Johnson**
Memorandum: 9 Mar 1702 examination of **Mary Hambleton** by **William Hutchison** and **John Hawkins**
Vide ye alienation in folio 83

- *folio 58a* • Indenture, 3 Mar 1702
From: **Coll. Henry Darnall**, of Prince George's County as agent for Charles, Lord Baltimore
To: **Charles Walker**, planter of Prince George's County
   London, 28 Nov 1691 His Lordship empowered **Henry Darnall** to "let" his land in Maryland. For the sum of 4£ he leased 200 acres of land in *Westerne Branch Manner* in Prince George's County bounded by land of **James Mullican** to **Charles Walker** for the natural life of he, his wife **Rebecca Walker** and **Elizabeth Walker**, his daughter for a yearly rent of 20 shillings and 2 capons, to plant and maintain an orchard of 430 apple tress and keep good repair of fences and enclosures.
Signed: **Henry Darnall**
Witnessed: **Clement Hill, Junior** and **Philip Darnall**
Alienation: 1 Feb 1702/3 Rec'd of **Thomas Clegett, Jr.** the sum of 5s
Vide ye conveyance in folio 7

JUNE COURT 1703
Att a Prince George's County Court held at Charles Town the 22 June 1703
for our Sovereign Lady Ann by the Grace of God Queen of England, Scottland, France and Ireland Defender of the faith and by her Majesties Justices appointed and authorized (VIZ)
William Hutchison   John Wight   Robert Bradly   Robert Tyler   William Tannyhill
Robert Wade   Thomas Sprigg   Samuel Magruder   James Stoddart

---

- *folio 60* • Indenture, 31 Dec 1702
From: **Jonathan Simons**, tailor of Prince George's County
To: **George Jones** of Prince George's County
   For 6,000 pounds of good tobacco **Johnathan Simons** and his wife **Elizabeth Simons** sold part of a parcel of land called *Quick Saile* containing 77 acres and 35 acres part of a tract called *Archers Pasture* lying in Prince George's County on the west side of the Patuxent; bounded by Taylor's Creek in a line with land of **Samuel Taylor**
Signed: **Johnathan Simmons** and **Elizabeth Simmons** (her mark)
Witnessed: **Tho. Greenfeild** and **Thomas Lude**
Endorsement: On back of deed 31 Dec 1702 **Elizabeth Simmons** examined by **Thom. Hollyday** and **William Barton**
Alienation: The sum of 1s/16p paid on 31 Dec 1702

• *folio 60a* • To All Christian People, 23 Jun 1703
From: **Josiah Willson** of Prince George's County, Gent.
To: **George Spicer** of Prince George's County
   George Spicer paid 80£ for a quit-claim deed to *Mansfeild* of 250 acres mentioning **Benjamin Evans** and a parcel called *Collins Comfort* containing 250 acres and another parcel called *The Farme* of 309 acres
Signed: **Josiah Willson**
Witnessed: **Rob. Tyler, Tho. Greenfeild** and **John Hawkins**

• *folio 61* • Indenture, 23 Jun 1703
From: **George Spicer**, planter of Prince George's County
To: **Joshua Cecell** of Prince George's County
   120£ for all of the tract of 309 acres called *The Farme* formerly in Calvert County and now in Prince George's County on the west side of the Patuxent in the woods at the head of a deep creek adjoining land granted **Thomas Truman** called *Mansfeild* and bounded by 100 acres of land of **William Selby** being part of the land called *The Farme*
Signed: **George Spicer**
Endorsement: 23 Jun 1703 **Mary Spicer**, wife of George, examined by **Robert Tyler** and **John Hawkins**
Witnessed: **Tho. Greenfeild, Robert Tyler** and **John Hawkins**
Alienation: The sum of 6s rec'd 23 Jun 1703 from **Joshua Cecell**

• *folio 62a* • Indenture, 4 Apr 1703
From: **Ninian Beall** of Prince George's County, Gent. and **Ruth**, his wife
To: **John Pottinger**, planter of Prince George's County
   For 105£ a parcel of 150 acres of land called *Twice Bought* being part of 800 acres of land surveyed for Beall called *Major's Lott* lying in Prince George's County, formerly Calvert County, in the fork of Western Branch; bounded by land owned by Pottinger
Signed: **Ninian Beall** and **Ruth Beall**
Witnessed: **Josiah Willson, Will'm Moor** (mark)
Memorandum: 10 Apr 1703 **Ruth Beall** examined by **William Hutchison** and **Robert Tyler**
Alienation: 10 Apr 1703 the sum of 6s paid by **John Pottinger**

• *folio 63a* • Indenture, 9 Apr 1703
From: **Edward Dawson**, planter of Prince George's County and wife **Mary Dawson**
To: **John Pottinger**, planter of Prince George's County
   For 70£ for 100 acres called *Ware* part of a tract called *The Majors Lott* in Prince George's County laid out for **Maj. Ninian Beall** by patent of 800 acres lying in the forks of the Western Branch of the Patuxent River; bounded by land of **James Millikin** and **John Joyce**
Signed: **Edward Dawson** and **Mary Dawson**
Witnessed: **Josiah Willson** and **Wm. Moore**
Memorandum: 10 Apr 1703 **Mary Dawson** examined by **Wm. Hutchison**
Alienation: **John Pottinger** paid the sum of 4s

• *folio 64* • Indenture, 14 Aug 1703
From: **Robert Johnson**, planter of Prince George's County and his wife **Elizabeth**
To: **Joshua Cecell** of Prince George's County
   100 acres of land called *Cuckold's Rest*, home of **Thomas Hide** at the time of his death lying in Calvert County, now Prince George's County, according to his will written 6 Feb 1697 made **Joannah Hide,** execx.; he left this land to his wife during her natural life, then to be divided between his two daughters, **Mary** and **Elizabeth**. The Widow Hide married **Bartholomew Goff** and daughter Elizabeth married **Robert Johnson**; no further mention of **Mary Hide**. Elizabeth sold 1/2 of the land to **Joshua Cecell** for 1,700 pounds of good tobacco
Signed: **Robert Johnson** (mark) and **Elizabeth Johnson** (mark)
Witnessed: **James Stoddart, Thomas Herneley,** and **Chr'r Baynes**
Memorandum: 14 Aug 1703 **Elizabeth Johnson** examined before **R. Bradly** and **James Stoddart**
Vide ye alienation in folio 97

13

- *folio 65a* • Indenture, 10 Apr 1703
From: **James Mullikin**, planter of Prince George's County, and his wife **Jane**
To: **Thomas Lemar**, planter of Prince George's County
    For 95£ a 100 acre parcel called *Thrice Bought* formerly called *Mullikin's Choice* in Prince George's County, formerly Calvert County, being part of 800 acres in the freshes of the Patuxent River in the fork of the Western Branch; bounded by *Major's Lott*
Signed: **James Mullikan** (mark), **Jane Mullikan** (mark)
Witnessed: **Josiah Willson** and **Wm. Moor** (mark)
Memorandum: 10 Apr 1703 **Jane Mullikin** examined by **William Hutchison** and **Robert Tyler**
Alienation: **Thomas Lemarr** paid the sum of 4s

- *folio 66* • Indenture, 24 Aug 1703
From: **Thomas Emmes**, mariner of the City of London
To: **James Stoddart** of Prince George's County, Gent.
    For 150£ a 163 acre parcel of land of *Mount Calvert Mannor* on the west side of the Patuxent River near the dividing of the river by a great marsh; bounded by *Spanish Oaks* of **John Deakins** land, part of said Manor, by **Christopher Bayne**, and by the main road to town; also including one acre of said Manor sold by **William Greene** while said Manor was in his possession to **Josias Towgood** for 99 years and 1 acre sold by Emmes and **David Small** to **James Stoddart** for 99 years and 5 acres of land laid out for use of the church and courthouse and one acre said Emmes reserves for himself
Signed: **Thomas Emmes**
Witnessed: **John Baldwin** and **Thomas Wells**

- *folio 67* • Indenture, 24 Aug 1703
From: **Luke Gardiner, Sr.** of St. Mary's County, Gent.
To: **John Geiles**, planter of Anne Arundel County
    For 90£ a tract of land in Charles County, now in Prince George's County called *Good Luck* of 780 acres of **Zachiriah Wade** and Luke and their heirs by virtue of a grant by the Right Honorable Lord Proprietor; Luke died before division made and said Zachiriah owned the entire tract by right of survivorship; in accord with an understanding made between them before Luke's death, Zachiriah left 1/2 the tract to **Theodotia Wade**, daughter of Zachariah; the other half portion went to the heirs of Luke and became the right of **Luke Gardiner, Jr.** of St. Mary's County and by him sold 1/2 the tract to above **Luke Gardiner, Sr.**
Signed: **Luke Gardiner, Sr.**
Witnessed: **Samuel Magruder** and **Thomas Sprigg, Jr.**
Memorandum: 24 Aug 1703 wife **Elizabeth Gardiner** examined by same
Recorded: 24 Aug 1703 for the sum of 9s for 525 acres

- *folio 67a* • Indenture, 4 Jan 1702
From: **Luke Gardiner, Sr.** of St. Mary's County, Gent.
To: **James Beall**, planter of Prince Georges County
    The other portion of 225 acres of the 780 acre property called *Good Luck* described in folio 67 left to **Theodotia Gardiner** now owned by **Luke Gardiner, Sr.** containing 223 acres for 90£
Signed: **Luke Gardiner, Sr.**
Witnessed: **Samuel Magruder** and **Thomas Sprigg, Junior**
Alienation: 29 Aug 1702 **James Beall** paid the sum of 9s for 225 acres

---

SEPTEMBER COURT 1703

Att a Prince George's County Court held at Charles Towne the 28th day of September 1703 for Sovereign Ann of England, Scotland, France and Ireland Queen by Her Majesties Justices thereunto authorized and appointed

Wm. Hutchison	John Wight	Robert Tyler	Will'm Tannyhill
Robert Wade	Sam'll Magruder	James Stoddart	Thomas Sprigg

• *folio 68a* • Letter of Attorney, 15 Sep 1703
From: **Daniell Burges** of the Parish of Sitteburne in the County of Richmond, Colony of Virginia
To: **Murphy Ward** of Prince George's County
  Mr. Burges appointed Mr. Ward his attorney to act for him in Prince George's County
Signed: **Dan'll Burges** (mark)
Witnessed: **Patrick Keely** (mark), **Peter Evans** and **Elizabeth Evans** (mark)
Recorded: September Court 1703

• *folio 69* • Indenture, 28 Sep 1703
From: **John Yale** of Baltimore County, Gent.
To: **John Mordock**, merchant of Prince George's County
  Paid 40£ for 340 acres of land lying in Prince George's County on the west side of the north branch of the Patuxent River being part of a tract of land called *Padsworth Farm;* bounded by **Richard Taylor**, Beaver Brooke, land laid out for **Thomas Bowdle**, and a tract called *Essington*
Signed: **John Yale**
Witnessed: **Tho. Clegett** and **Edw. Holmes**
Acknowledged: 28 Sep 1703 by **Robert Tyler** and **Tho. Sprigg**
Vide ye alienation in folio 100 of this book

• *folio 69a* • Indenture, 26 Mar 1703
From: **William Barton** of Prince George's County, Gent.
To: **Richard Marsham** of Prince George's County
  Bowling's Neck sold for 70£ and 150 acre part of a tract called *Marsham's Rest*; on west side of Patuxent and south side of mouth of Deep Creek
Signed: **William Barton**
Acknowledgment: **Sarah Barton** examined 19 Mar 1702 by **John Wight** and **Robert Bradly**

NOVEMBER COURT 1703
Att a Prince George's County Court held at Charles Town the 24th of November 1703
for our Sovereign Lady Ann by the Grace of God Queen of England, Scottland, France and
Ireland Defender of the faith and by her Majesties Justices appointed and authorized (VIZ)

• *folio 70a* • Indenture, 26 Mar 1703
From: **Richard Marsham** of Prince George's County, Gent.
To: **William Barton** of Prince George's County
  Bowling Neck, a 200 acre parcel, purchased for 70£ and 150 acre part of land called *Marsham's Rest*; bounded by land formerly sold by **Richard Marsham** to **Thomas Gannt** and now in possession of **Mr. John Wight**; and by land called *The Exchange*; Royal mines excepted
Signed: **Richard Marsham**
Endorsement: 19 Mar 1702/3 **Ann Marsham**, wife of Richard, examined by **John Wight** and **R. Bradly**
Recorded: 18 Dec 1703 by **Wm. Barton**, alienation 3s

• *folio 71a* • Indenture, 30 Jul 1703
From: **John Soaper**, cooper of Prince George's County
To: **John Lewis**, planter of Prince George's County
  Nicholas Terrill, dec'd, of Anne Arundel County sold **Thomas Hillary**, dec'd, of Calvert County land lying then in Calvert now Prince George's County on the north side of Western Branch of the Patuxent River called *Marborrow's Plains*; Terrill did not sign over to Hillary, then sold to Soaper; Soaper dissatisfied and relinquished to Hillary the southeast one-half of the land; then Hillary sold said 1/2 to **John Lewis** but Hillary had no conveyance; southeast corner of land on Cabin Branch
Signed: **John Soaper** (mark) and **Mary Soaper** (mark) his wife
Endorsement: 30 Jul 1703 **Mary Soaper** examined by **Robert Wade** and **Samuel Magruder**
Witnessed: **Thomas Clagett** and **John Rigdon**
Alienation: 18 Dec 1703 for the sum of 6s from **John Lewis**

JANUARY COURT 1703
Att a Prince George's County Court held at Charles Towne the 25th of January 1703
by her Majesties Justices thereunto authorized and appointed VIZ
Wm. Hutchison   John Wight   Robert Bradly   Robert Tyler
John Hawkins   Rob't Wade   Sam'll Magruder   Thomas Sprigg   James Stoddart

• *folio 72A* • Indenture, 2 Jun 1703
From: **Luke Gardiner**, the elder, of St. Mary's County, Gent.
To: **John Mason**, son of **Robert Mason**, late of St. Mary's Co., now residing in London in Old England
   For 18,000 pounds of tobacco paid by the late **Robert Mason** to **Luke Gardiner** for 580 acres of land called *Grimes Ditch* formerly in Charles County now in Prince George's County on the north side of the Potomac River near Mattawoman; bounded by *St. John's Value* being the northernmost bounds of land formerly of **Capt. Thomas Cornwallis** near an Indian field; containing an island in the Potomac River; granted 20th Feb 1693 by **Cecillius, Lord Baltimore** to **Robert Mason** in his lifetime and by his last will to **John Mason**
Signed: **Luke Gardiner, Sr.**
Witnessed: **Nicholas Genlick, Jos. Vanswaringen,** and **Tho. Grunwin**
Acknowledged: 2 Jun 1703 by **Luke Gardiner** to **Henry Lowe** and **John Nutthall**
St. Mary's County Court acknowledged this deed signed by **G. Muschamp**
Vide ye alienation in folio 83

• *folio 73a* • Indenture, 24 Jun 1703
From: **Col. Ninean Beal** of Prince George's County, Gent., and **Ruth Beal**
To: **Thomas Beall**, carpenter of Prince George's County
   For a competent sum of money sold 490 acre part of 1,673 acres *Addition to Caverton Edge* granted Beall on 20 Dec 1694; Condition of Plantation 5 Apr 1684; certificate in land office 19 Jun 1695
Signed: **Ninian Beall**
Witnessed: **Obadyah Kernby** and **William Shepard**
Endorsement: 24 Jun 1703 **Ruth Beall** examined by **Sam'll Mason** and **Wm. Tannyhill**
Signed: **Wm. Tannyhill** and **Sam'll Magruder**

• *folio 74a* • Indenture, 23 Dec 1703
From: **Elizabeth Ellott**, widow, execx. of **Dall Ellott**, late of Prince George's County
To: **Richard Jarrell** of Prince George's County
   100 acre part of a tract called *Denn* near the Eastern Branch of the Potomac River bounded by **Francis Prissley's** land called *Forgot* and land owned by **Ninian Beall**
Signed: **Elizabeth Ellott** (mark)
Witnessed: **Tho's Fletchall, Andrew Hamblelon** and **James Riggs**
Acknowledgement: **Elizabeth Ellott** examined by **John Addison** and **Wm. Tannyhill**
Alienation: 18 Mar 1703 the sum of 4s paid by **Richard Jarrell**

• *folio 75* • Indenture, 23 Feb 1702
From: **Charles Eagerton** of St. Mary's County
To: **James Heath** of Kent County, Gent.
   For 125£ a 600 acre part of 3,000 acres granted by **Cecillius, Lord Baltimore** to **William Calvert, Esq'r** on 11 Feb 1662; located on the east side of Piscattawy River and south side of creek called Piscattaway; bounded by **Randolfe Hanson**; near the Indian fort
Signed: **Charles Egarton**
Witnessed: **R. Llewelling** and **Jos. Vanswaringen**
Acknowledged: 23 Feb 1703 before St. Mary's County officials; signed **Thos. Beall & Jno. Baker**
Alienation: 23 Feb 1702 memorandum of 600 acres due
Recorded: St. Mary's County by **R. Llewelling**
Recorded: Prince George's County by **James Heath** of Anne Arundel Co., Gent.

16

(Ed: note that the first part of the document says he is from Kent County.)
Survey: Land called *Capt. John's Neck* bounded by **Francis Marbry**; signed by **Wm. Hutchison**, Surveyor; and acknowledged by him 15 Feb 1703

• *folio 76* • Indenture, 15 Feb 1703
From: **Hugh Ryley** of Prince George's County
To: **Edward Dawson** of Prince George's County
   For 134£ a 510 acre tract of land called *Ryley's Discovery* (now called *Ware Park*) lying in Prince George's County; bounded by Back Branch and *Ryley's Discovery*
Signed: **Hugh Ryley**
Now called *Ware Park* between the 10th & 11th line, interlined before & signed in presence of us **Richard Duckett** and **Thomas Ricketts**
Memorandum: 15 Feb 1703 **Hugh Ryley** and his wife **Mary** acknowledged deed
Signed: **John Wight** and **Thomas Sprigg, Jr.**
Alienation: 15 Feb 1703 the sum of 8s/5p paid by **Edward Davison**

• *folio 77* • Indenture, 15 Feb 1703
From: **Hugh Ryley**, carpenter of Prince George's County
To: **Thomas Ricketts** of Anne Arundel County
   For 266£ a 380 acre tract of land being part of the 1,000 acres of *Ryley's Discovery*; bounded by the plantation of **Matthew Mackebey** and land laid out for **Major Nicholas Sewell** and **John Darnall, Esq'r**; by *Major's Lott* and Back Branch
Signed: **Hugh Ryley**
Endorsed: **Richard Duckett** and **Edward Dawson**
Memorandum: Endorsed 15 Feb 1703; **Mary Ryley** examined by **Jno. Wight** and **Tho's Sprigg, Jr.**
Alienation: 15 Feb 1703 the sum of 15s/3p paid by **Thomas Ricketts**

• *folio 78* • Indenture, 15 Feb 1703
From: **Charles Cheyney**, planter of Anne Arundel County
To: **Justinian Bazwell**, planter of Anne Arundel County
   For 41£ a 50 acre tract of land called *Cheeneys Beginning*, part of a tract called *Cheeneys Adventure* lying "on the other side of the Patuxent River" in Prince George's County
Signed: **Charles Cheeney** (mark)
Endorsement: **Richard Duckett** and **Thomas Ricketts**
Memorandum: 15 Feb 1703 **Ann Cheeney** examined by **John Wight** and **Thomas Sprigg**
Alienation: 15 Feb 1703 the sum of 2s paid by **Justinian Bazwell**

• *folio 79* • Indenture, 16 Feb 1704
From: **Coll. Ninian Beall** of Prince George's County
To: **Arch'd Edmundson**, carpenter of Prince George's County
   Dunkell, formerly in Calvert County, now in Prince George's County, from a tract of land containing 1,440 acres granted Beall by **John Scott** of Calvert County dated 26 Aug 1696; 150 acres called *Dunkell* sold for 7,000 pounds of tobacco; bounded by *Swanson's Land* and **Anthony Smith's** land
Signed: **Ninian Beall**
Witnessed: **Clement Davis** and **John Geiles**
Endorsement: 16 Feb 1703 **Ruth Beall** examined by **Robert Wade** and **Sam'll Magruder**
Alienation: 16 Feb 1703 the sum of 6s paid by **Archibald Edmundson**

• *folio 80* • Indenture, 16 Feb 1704
From: **Coll. Ninian Beall** of Prince George's County
To: **Archibald Edmundson**, carpenter of Prince George's County
   179 acres of land called *The Gore* for 3,200 pounds of tobacco; bounded by **Christopher Thompson** on the south side of the Eastern Branch of the Potomac River; plus 21 acres of Beall's land called *The Meadows*
Signed: **Ninian Beall**
Witnessed: **Clement Davis** and **John Geiles**

17

Endorsement: 16 Feb 1703 **Ruth Beall** examined by **Rob't Wade** and **Sam'll Magruder**
Alienation: 16 Feb 1703 the sum of 8s paid by **Archibald Edmundson**

• *folio 80A* • Indenture, 11 Mar 1703/4
From: **Thomas Loyd**, planter of Prince George's County
To: **Sam'll, Joseph,** and **Hannah Coapland** of Prince George's County
    For 54£/5s/2p a tract of 52 acres; bounded by **Samuel Taylor's** land formerly purchased by Loyd from Taylor
Warrant: **Thomas Loyd** agrees to pay **Samuel** and **Joseph Coapland** 18£/1s/8p & a half-penny when they reach the age of 21 and pay **Hannah Coapland** the same at age 16 or on her marriage day
Signed: **Thomas Loyd**
Witnessed: **Edward Willett** and **Josh Hall**
Memorandum: Acknowledgement before **Robert Bradley** and **James Stoddart**

• *folio 81a* • Indenture, 15 Jan 1703
From: **Charles Egerton** of St. Mary's County, Gent., and **Mary**, his wife
To: **James Heath** of Anne Arundel County
    For 125£ a 600 acre tract of land, part of 3,000 acres in Prince George's County on the east side of the Piscattaway River and the south side of Piscattaway Creek; bounded by land of **Randolph Henson** and a ashen swamp creek near an Indian field. On 11 Feb 1662 **William Calvert, Esq'r,** dec'd, gave 600 of this 3,000 acres to his daughter **Elizabeth** when she married **James Neale** of Charles County, Gent. **Charles Calvert,** son and heir of **William Calvert,** for valuable consideration sold the remaining 2,400 acres to **Charles Egerton,** deceased, father to the said Charles named above; bounded by land of **Cap. Johns Heck, Francis Marburie,** and land where old Piscattaway Fort stood
Signed: **Cha. Egerton** and **Mary Egerton**
Witnessed: **C. Butler, George Mason, Ralph Heirrison**
Memorandum: St. Mary's County 10 Mar 1703 **Mary Egerton** was examined by **John Nutthall** and **Josh Guybert**; certified by **Geo. Muschamp**, Clerk, St. Mary's County
Alienation: 14 Mar 1703 alienation for 600 acres due **James Heath**, Clerk

• *folio 82a* • Vide ye conveyance in folio 73; 9 Mar 1703 rec'd of **John Mason** the sum of 3s/2p & a halfe-penny alienation of the land from **Luke Gardiner**

• *folio 82a* • Vide ye conveyance in folio 58; 12 Sep 1703 from **Wm. Tannyhill** 4s/11p for alienation of the deed for acc't of **James Heath**

• *folio 82a* • Indenture, 20 Feb 1702/3
From: **Thomas Brooke** of Prince George's County, Esq'r
To: **Thomas Wall**, planter of Prince George's Count
    For 4,900 pounds of good merchantable tobacco for 70 acres part of land called *Brookefeild* lying in Prince George's County west of the Patuxent River in the freshes between the branches of Mattapany Creek and Deep Creek; bounded by land taken up by **Nathaniel Trumen**: Royal mines excepted
Signed: **Thomas Brooke**
Witnessed: _____ **Smith** and **Wm. Barton**
Memorandum: 20 Feb 1700 (sic), **Madame Barbara Brooke**, wife of said Thomas, examined by **Tho. Greenfeild** and **Jno. Wight**
Alienation: 20 Feb 1700 (sic) the sum of 1s/6p paid for 70 acres by **Thomas Wall**

• *folio 83a* • Indenture, 28 Mar 1704
From: **John Smith** of Charles County
To: **Thomas Gibbins,** planter of Prince George's County
    For 5,300 pounds of tobacco in cask 50 acres of land called *Smith's Green* lying in Prince George's County; bounded by *Smith's Pasture* and land called *Shoake*
Signed: **John Smith**
Witnessed: **Edward Willett** and **Ro't Owen**

18

Memorandum: 28 Mar 1704 **Ann Smith,** wife of John, examined by **John Wight** and **Sam'll Magruder**
Vide ye alienation in folio 94

• *folio 84a* • 25 Oct 1703
From: **Kessin Casseyous,** Queen of Pamunkey
To: **William Hutchison** of Prince George's County
     "For 200 armes length of Roanoake" and for "diverse other considerations" a tract of land lying in Prince George's County on Pamunkey Creek "bought of us on which he hath seated a plantation" bounded by Licking Bank Branch containing 250 acres for the natural life of **William** and **Sarah Hutchison**, his wife, and for the life of his son, **John Hutchison**; to be returned to me, my heirs and successors
Signed: **Kessin Casseyous** (mark)
Witnessed: **Fre. Wheeler** and **Thomas Fandry**
Memorandum: 25 Oct 1703 the Queen of Pamunkey came before **William Hatton**, appointed by the Assembly to take acknowledgement of Indians selling land to English

• *folio 84a* • 25 Mar 1702
From: **Luke Gardiner, Junior,** of St. Mary's County, Gent.
To: **Luke Gardiner, Senior**
     Luke, Jr. signs over this rights to one-half of a parcel of land lying in the woods on the back of **Walter Evans** known as *Good Luck*; taken up by his grandfather, **Capt. Luke Gardiner** of St. Mary's County and **Zachariah Waid** of Charles County of 750 acres in Prince George's County; assigned to his uncle **Luke Gardiner** of St. Mary's County, Gent.
Signed: 6 Sep 1701 by **Luke Gardiner, Jr.**
Witnessed: **Cornelius Branair** and **John Gardiner**
Assignment on back: **Luke Gardiner, Jr.,** assigned 1/2 of *Good Luck* to **Thomas Sprigg** and **John Giles** on 25 Mar 1702
Signed: **Luke Gardiner, Sr.**
Witnessed: **James Brooke** and **Charles Ridgely**
Assignment by **Thomas Sprigg, Jr.** to **James Beall** of above land; all preceding assignments put on record at the request of **James Beall**

• *folio 85* • Indenture, 26 Oct 1703
From: **Thomas Brooke, Esq'r** of Prince George's County
To: **Thomas Blandford,** planter of Prince George's County
     For 30£ a 209 acre parcel of a tract of land called *Brooke Chance* in Prince George's County; bounded by Brooke Creek
Signed: **Thos. Brooke**
Witnessed: **Wm. Hutchison** and **Josiah Willson**
Memorandum: 16 Oct 1703 **Thomas Brooke, Esq'r** came before **Wm. Hutchison** and **James Stoddart** acknowledging deed
Memorandum: 29 Oct 1703 **Madam Barbara Brooke,** wife of Thomas, acknowledged deed before **John Wight** and **Rob't Bradly**
Alienation: 26 Oct 1703 the sum of 8s/4p paid by **Thomas Blandford**

• *folio 86* • Indenture, 11 Aug 1703
From: **Ignatius Craycroft** of Prince George's County, Gent.
To: **Joshua Cecell** of Prince George's County
     John Craycroft, joyner of Calvert County, dec'd, during his lifetime granted a 450 acre tract of land called *Craycroft's Right* lying in Calvert County now Prince George's County to **Ignatius Craycroft**; lying on the west side of the Patuxent; bounded by an Indian field, and a parcel of land formerly laid out for Craycroft called *Heathorne Heath*; all but 199 acres found to be part of His Lordship's *Manor of Calverton* by certificate of survey made by **James Thompson,** Dept'y Surveyor under **Baker Brook, Esq'r,** Surveyor General, dated 16 Feb 1675 according to records of the Provincial Court; the 199 acres not contained in the older survey of *Calverton Manor* sold to **Joshua Cecell** for 57£.

Signed: **Ignatius Craycroft**
Memorandum: 30 Sep 1703 **Sophia Craycroft** examined by **Jno. Wight** and **Rob't Bradly**
Witnessed: **George Smyth** (mark), **James Grah** (mark), **John Wight, R. Bradly**
Alienation: 10 Jun 1704 the sum of 8s paid by **Joshua Cecell**

• folio 87a • Indenture, 1 Nov 1703
From: **Robert** and **Margery Horton** of St. Mary's County; Margery being the former **Margery Gardiner**, relict of **Richard Gardiner**, late of St. Mary's County, but before division of the counties called Calvert County
To: **Joshua Cecell** of Prince George's County
    On 10 Jan 1680 by His Lordship's grant (record still remaining in the Land Office) a certain tract of land in Calvert County now in Prince George's County called *The Margery* containing 200 acres was given to **Richard Gardiner**; by the will dated 15 Jan 1693 willed the land to his wife, Margery; an error in the grant was corrected by Condition of Plantation record dated 1684 and remaining on record in the Land Office; lying on the west side of Western Branch of the Patuxent River; bounded by land of **Alexander Magruder** and **Capt. Richard Ladd**; Royal mines excluded; 200 acres sold for 30£
Signed: **Robert Hourton** and **Margery Hourton** (mark)
Memorandum: 1 Nov 1703 **Margery Horton** examined by **Ralph Hoster** and **James Swann**
St. Mary's County: Hoster and Swann acknowledge said deed before **George Muschamp**, Clerk
Alienation: 10 Jun 1704 the sum of 8s paid by **Joshua Cecell**

• *folio 89a* • Indenture, 27 Mar 1703
From: **John Miller**, planter of Prince George's County and **Ann**, his wife
To: **Roger Brooke** of Calvert County, Gent.
    For valuable consideration 130 acres of land called *Hazard* formerly granted **William Barton** of Calvert County now lying in Prince George's County in the woods at the NW corner of *Brookewood*
Signed: **John Miller** and **Ann Miller** (mark)
Witnessed: **Samuel Magruder** and **James Stoddart**
Memorandum: 27 Mar 1703 **John** and **Ann Miller** acknowledged deed before same witnesses
Vide ye alienation in folio 153

MARCH COURT 1704
Att a Prince George's County Court held at Charles Towne the 28th day of March for our Sovereign Lady Ann Queen of England, Scottland, France and Ireland Queen defender of the faith by her Majesties Justices thereunto authorized and appointed Annoq Dom 1704

William Hutchison	Robert Bradly	John Wight	Robert Tyler
William Tanyhill	Samuell Magruder	Thomas Sprigg	James Stoddart

---

• *folio 90* • Indenture, 15 Feb 1703
From: **Hugh Ryley**, carpenter of Prince George's County
To: **Thomas Ricketts**, planter of Anne Arundel County
    For 266£ a tract of 380 acres of land part of *Ryley's Discovery* in Prince George's County; bounded by plantation of **Matthew Mackeboy** and land formerly laid out for **Major Nicholas Sewell** and **John Darnall, Esq'r**; adjoining *Major's Lott, Something,* and Back Branch
Signed: **Hugh Ryley**
Memorandum: **Mary Ryley**, wife of Hugh, examined by **John Wight** and **Thomas Sprigg, Jr.**
Witnessed: **Richard Duckett** and **Edward Dawson**
Alienation: 15 Feb 1703 the sum of 15s paid by **Thomas Ricketts**

• *folio 91* • Indenture, 13 Feb 1703
From: **Hugh Ryley** of Prince George's County, Gent.
To: **Richard Isaac**, planter of Prince George's County

For 75£ a 150 acre parcel of land called *Stoney Plaines* part of a tract of land called *Ryley's Range* of 800 acres; bounded by land laid out for **John Baptistyler** and *Darnall's Grove*; Royal mines excepted
Signed: **Hugh Ryley**
Endorsement: 15 Apr 1703 his wife **Mary Ryley** examined by **John Wight** and **Thomas Sprigg**
Witnesses: **Charles Ridgely** and **Jonathan Simmon**
Alienation: 27 Feb 1703 the sum of 6s paid by **Richard Isaac**

* *folio 92* • Indenture, 15 Feb 1703
From: **Hugh Ryley** of Prince George's County, Gent.
To: **Richard Isaac**, planter of Prince George's County
For only 5£ a 150 acre part of land called *Newfound Land* in Prince George's County; bounded by *Darnall's Grove* and the original tract of *Good Luck*; Royal mines excepted
Signed: **Hugh Ryley**
Endorsement: 15 Feb 1703 **Mary Ryley**, wife of Hugh, examined by **John Wight** and **Thomas Sprigg, Jr.**
Alienation: The sum of 6s paid on 27 Feb 1703 by **Richard Isaac**

* *folio 92a* • Indenture, 25 Mar 1704
From: **Coll. Ninian Beall** of Prince George's County, Gent.
To: **John Cole** of Prince George's County
For 35£ a 160 acre tract called *The Inclosure* in Prince George's County near the Eastern Branch of the Potomac River; bounded by land of **Andrew Tannyhill** and **William Tannyhill**
Endorsement: **Ruth Beall** examined by **Robert Bradly** and **James Stoddart**
Alienation: 29 Mar 1704 the sum of 6s paid by **John Cole**
Witnessed: **Robert Bradly** and **James Stoddart**

* *folio 93a* • Vide ye conveyance folio 84; 14 Apr 1704 **Thomas Gibbons** paid 4s

* *folio 93a* • Indenture, 12 Dec 1702
From: **James Thompson**, salesman of Shaftsbury in the County of Dorcett
To: **William Tannyhill**, planter of Prince George's County
For 25£ a 184 acre tract of land called *Phillip Lough* in Charles County now in Prince George's County; on the northwest branch of the Eastern Branch of the Potomc; bounded by *Manor of Zechia*
Signed: **James Thompson**
Memorandum: 17 Dec 1702, signed **Sam. Dasewood**, Major
Witnessed: **James Wallace** and **Hickford Leman**
Acknowledged in open court and also acknowledge by Letter of Attorney from **James Thompson**
Alienation: 29 Mar 1704 the sum of 11s/4p paid by **William Tanyhill**

* *folio 94* • Petition, 23 Mar 1702/3
Resurvey of *Major's Lott* in Prince George's County
Petitioners: **Edward Dawson, James Mullikin, Mathew Mackeby**, and the executors of **John Joyce**
To: **Josiah Wilson**, High Sheriff of Prince George's County and **Mr. William Hutchison**, Surveyor
Bounds: Land of **Maj. Nicholas Sewell, Edward Dawson, John Pottinger, James Mullikin, Thomas Lemarr, Matthew Mackeby**
Her Majesties' Surveyor: **William Hutchison**
Signed: Jury included **Thomas Swaringen, Richard Pile, Archibald Edmundson, Thomas Plumer** (mark)**, Charles Hyatt, John Turner** (mark)**, Anthony Draine, Soloman Rodery, Jonathan Simmons, Wm. Ray** (mark)**, William Moor** (mark)**, Thomas Wells**

* *folio 95* • Petition, 20 Apr 1703
Resurvey of *St. Elizabeth* in Prince George's County
Petitioner: **Nathaniell Magruder**
Resurvey to define land left Magruder's wife from the will of the late **Geiles Blizard** of Charles County called *Bero Plains* which was taken away by **Col. John Addison** in a resurvey of

21

St. Elizabeth: bounds **George Thompson**, the river (unnamed), **Col. John Addison**, St. John's Creek; **Thomas Locker** identified one "bounded tree" he had known for 16 years
Signed: 6 May 1703 **John Hawkins, Robert Wade, Charles Ridgly, Robert Brooke, John Miller, Robert Middleton, Henry Cullver, James Beall, Henry Gutterick, Francis Marbury, Thomas Edlin,** and **Wallter Bryne**
Her Majesties' Surveyor: **William Hutchison**

* *folio 96* • Petition, 20 Nov 1703
Resurvey of *Tuexbury* in Prince George's County
Petitioner: **Robert Tyler**
Bounded: The oath of **Hugh Ryley** says **John Mootree** informed him **Col. Ninian Beall** showed him and **Robert Jones** "northwest corner tree of tract called *Scott's Lott*"; *Resurvey of Cheroxbury*; near Collington Branch; found to contain 184 acres
Signed: **Archibald Edmundson, John Pottinger, Edward Holmes, Thomas Wells, Hugh Abrahams, John Ramsey, Thomas Box, Thomas Pindle** (mark), **Robert Anderson** (mark), **Thomas Plumer** (mark), **Charles Hyatt**
Her Majesties' Surveyor: **William Hutchison**

* *folio 96* • Petition, 18 Oct 1703
Resurvey of *Chelsey* in Prince George's County
Petitioner: **Christopher Thompson** for the third interest of his wife, formerly **Grace Williams** widow of the late **James Williams, Sr.** left her by her right of dower; bounded by Western Branch
Signed: **Hugh Ryley, Thomas Beall, Joshua Hall, Anthony Drayne, Benjamin Brasheers, Edward Holmes, Peter Seamper** (mark), **Thomas Willson** (mark), **Christopher Baynes, William Lee, John Mills** (mark), **William Ray** (mark)

* *folio 96* • Vide ye conveyance Liber A, folio 148 & 149; 3 Jun 1704 **Joshua Cecell** paid 3s for alienation of 150 acres part of *Collins Comfort*

* *folio 96* • Vide ye conveyance Liber A, folio 148 & 149; 23 Jun 1703 **Joshua Cecell** paid 6s/4p for alienation of *The Farme*

* *folio 96* • Vide ye conveyance in Liber (sic) 64 this book; 3 Jun 1704 **Joshua Cecill** paid 4s for alienation (of *Cuckold's Rest*)

* *folio 96a* • Indenture, 9 Dec 1703
From: **George Spicer** of Prince George's County
To: **Joshua Cecell** of Prince George's County
    For 60£ a tract of 150 acre part of a parcel of land called *Mansfeild* or part of a parcel called *Collings Comfort* or part of either or both as they may happen when just survey is made; bounded by Deep Creek
Signed: **George Spicer**
Memorandum: 1 May 1704 **Mary Spicer,** wife of George, examined by **R. Bradly** and **James Stoddart**
Witnessed: **Thomas Greenfeild** and **James Stoddart**
Alienation: 3 Jun 1704 the sum of 3 shillings paid by **Joshua Cecell**
Recorded: 10 Jun 1704

JUNE COURT 1704

Att Prince George's County Court held at Charles Towne the 27th day of June 1704 for our Sovereign Lady Ann by the Grace of God of England, Scottland, France and Ireland Queen defender of the faith and by her Majesties Justices thereunto authorized and appointed as, VIZ

William Barton	John Wight	Robert Bradly	Robert Tyler
William Tanyhill	Robert Wade	Sam'll Magruder	James Stoddart

- *folio 98* • Deed of Gift, 14 Jun 1704
From: **Thomas Brooke** of Prince George's County, Esq'r
To: **Major Dent, Esq'r**
    For the "natural love and affection that I have and do bear unto my well beloved daughter **Sarah Brooke** and for advancement in marriage and future support and maintenance" 500 acres of a great tract of land called *Dann* near where Rock Creek falls into the Potomac River in Prince George's County
Signed: **Thomas Brooke**
Witnessed: **Rich'd Marsham** and **R't Owen**
Endorsement: 14 Jun 1704 acknowledged by **Rebeckah Brooke**, wife of **Thomas**
(In the next folio the wife of Thomas Brooke is Madame Barbara Brooke)
Witnessed: **William Barton** and **John Wight**

- *folio 98a* • Indenture, 14 Oct 1703
From: **Thomas Brooke** of Prince George's County, Esq'r
To: **Nicholas Sewell** of St. Mary's County, Esq'r
    For 200£ an 862 acre tract of land of two parcels of adjoining land called *Brookefeild* and *Brooke Discovery* in Prince George's County on the west side of the Patuxent River in the freshes beginning "at a great bridge in a cart path"; bounded by the cart path, a plantation owned by Sewell where **James Watts** lives, to the tobacco house on another Sewell plantation to a land called *The Wedge* standing by the river, the Patuxent River, to an Indian Fort, to land of **Robert Armes**, to land of **John Smith** and to an Old Indian Path in a branch known as Bridge Branch
Signed: **Thomas Brooke**
Witnessed: **John Warren** and **Joshua Cecill**
Memorandum: 14 Oct 1703 **Madame Barbara Brooke** examined by **William Barton** and **Rob't Bradly**
(In the preceeding document the wife of Thomas Brooke is named Rebeckah Brooke)
Alienation: 27 Jun 1704 by **Nicholas Sewell**
Recorded: 3 Jul 1704

- *folio 100* • 1 Jul 1704 rec'd of **John Murdock** 13s/9p; Vide ye conveyance in folio 69 of this book

- *folio 100* • Indenture, 24 Mar 1703
From: **Col. Ninian Beall** of Prince George's County, Gent.
To: **Richard Weaver**, planter of Prince George's County
    For 6,000 pounds of good sound merchantable tobacco all 132 acres of a tract of land called *Chance* now called *Weaver's Purchase*; bounded by **Walter Evans** land, and the stream called Cabin Branch
Signed: **Ninian Beall**
Witnessed: **Rob. Bradly, James Stoddart** and **William Young**
Endorsement: 24 Mar 1703 **Ruth Beall** examined by **R. Bradly** and **James Stoddart**
Alienation: 1 Jul 1704 the sum of 5s paid by **Richard Weaver**
Recorded: 4 Jul 1704

- *folio 101* • Indenture, 12 Apr 1704
From: **William Collings** of Stafford County, Colony of Virginia
To: **Thomas Addison** of Prince George's County
    For 12£ and for diverse other good causes and considerations a 100 acre part of a parcel of land called *Quick Sale* lying in the freshes of the Patuxent River in Prince George's County; bounded by land of **Samuel Taylor**; one half part of *Quick Sale* (400 acres) was formerly sold by **Francis Street** to **William Collings** and given equally by the last will of **William Collins** to his sons, **William Collins** and **Moulton Collins**; at the death of **Moulton Collins** the land was inherited by **William Collings**, the elder brother
Signed: **William Collins** (mark)
Witnessed: **John Storry, Benj'n Scott**
Alienation: 1 Jul 1704 the sum of 2s paid by **Thomas Addison**

• *folio 101a* • Indenture, 28 Mar 1704
From: **Thomas Lemar,** planter of Prince George's County
To: **Charles Hyatt,** planter of Prince George's County
   For 35£ a 45 acre parcel of land in Prince George's County near Collington Branch; bounded by land of **Major Nicholas Sewell** and **John Darnall;** by **Charles Hayes'** Branch
Signed: **Thomas Lemar** and **Ann Lemar**
Endorsement: 28 Mar 1704 of **Thomas** and **Ann Lemar** before **Sam'll Magruder** and **Thomas Sprigg**
Witnessed: **Tho. Clogett** and **Tho. Swarington**
Alienation: 1 Jul 1704 the sum of 1s/9p paid by **Charles Hyatt**
Recorded: 7 Jul 1704

• *folio 102a* • Indenture, 27 Jun 1704
From: **Abraham Clark,** planter of Prince George's County
To: **Richard Tayler,** planter of Prince George's County
   For 12£ a 24 1/4 acre tract of land in Prince George's County on the west side of the north branch of the Patuxent River; bounded by *Essington*
Signed: **Abra. Clarke**
Endorsement: 27 Jun 1704 wife **Elizabeth Clarke** examined by **Robert Tyler** and **Sam'll Magruder**
Alienation: 1 Jul 1704 the sum of 6p paid by **Richard Tayler**
Witnessed: **John Murdock** and **Watt. Maynes**
Recorded: 7 Jul 1704

• *folio 103* • Indenture, 13 Jun 1704
From: **Phillip Gittings** of Prince George's County, Gent.
To: **Thomas Lucas,** planter of Prince George's County
   For 20£ a 20 acre parcel of land in Prince George's County; bounded by **Thomas Sprigg, Sr.**
Signed: **Phill. Gittings**
Witnessed: **Charles Ridgly** and **John Jackson**
Endorsement: 13 Jun 1704 wife **Ann Gittings** examined by **Rob't Tyler** and **Sam'll Magruder**
Alienation: 3 Jul 1704 the sum of 10p paid by **Thomas Lucas**
Recorded: 6 Jul 1704

• *folio 103a* • Obligation, 26 Jul 1704
From: **Charles Busey,** planter of Calvert County
To: **William Rothery,** tailor of Prince George's County
   Charles Busey binds himself to pay **William Rothery** 11,000 pounds of tobacco for the 100 acres of land called *Twyfoot* in Prince George's County which **William Selby,** dec'd, formerly sold to **William Downeing; Charles Busey** inherited from Downeing; Selby did not make lawful deed to Downeing in their lifetime; **William Rothery** paid 5,500 pounds of tobacco and "casks in hull" for the above land; when the heirs of **William Selby** come of age and make deed in fee simple to **William Rothery,** this obligation becomes void
Signed: **Charles Buesey**
Witnessed: **William Congley** and **Joshua Cecell**

• *folio 104* • Indenture, 28 Jun 1704
From: **Hickford Leman** of Prince George's County, Gent.
To: **Thomas Addison** of Prince George's County, Gent.
   For 265£/16s a 400 acre half-part of land called *Batchelor's Harbour* of 800 acres in Prince George's County, formerly Charles County on the east side of the Potomac about 2 miles above Piscataway Creek; bounded by Borge's Creek, Jerom's Creek, now known as Swann Creek, and St. George's Creek
Signed: **Hickford Leman**
Endorsed and witnessed: **Josiah Willson, Robert Middleton, James Haddock**
Alienation: 28 Jun 1704 the sum of 8s paid by **Thomas Addison**

24

• *folio 105a* • Indenture, 29 Jun 1704
From: **James Stoddart** of Prince George's County, Gent.
To: **Frederick Claudius** of Prince George's County, Chyrurgion (Ed: Surgeon)
For 150£ one 50 acre tract called *Long Looked For* in Prince George's County bounded by land called *Little Groave* belonging to **Maj. Thomas Brooke** on the main south branch of Deep Creek in line with land laid out for **Richard Marsham**; also a tract of 200 acres of land formerly granted to **Major Thomas Brooke** now in the possession of **Murphy Ward** and part of a 200 acre tract granted to Ward called *Ward's Pasture* in Prince George's County on the west side of the Patuxent in the woods in the branches of a neck called Deep Neck; bounded by *Long Looked For* belonging to **George Lingan**
Signed: **James Stoddert**
Witnessed: **Tho's Addison, Edward Willett,** and **Ja. Haddock**
Memorandum: 29 Jun 1704 wife **Mary Stoddart** examined by **Will. Tanyhill** and **Tho. Addison**
Alienation: 26 Jul 1704 the sum of 5s paid by **Frederick Caludius**
Recorded: 27 Aug 1704

• *folio 106a* • Deed of Gift, 27 Nov 1703
From: **Nicholas Sewell** of St. Mary's County, Gent.
To: **Clement Brooke** of Prince George's County and to **Jane,** his wife
"For natural love and affection I bear unto my son-in-law **Clement Brooke**" and to **Jane,** his wife, for settlement of their inheritance a 330 acre parcel of land lying in Prince George's County, part of a tract called *Brookefeild*; bounded by the Bridge Branch; to be given to those heirs of Clement and Jane which he, Clement, "shall think fit"; if no heirs of them then to any heirs of Jane; or if she should have no heirs then to the heirs of Clement
Signed: **Nicholas Sewell**
Witnessed: **Anthothy Moralie** and **Isaac Youell**
Memorandum: **Nicholas Sewell** acknowledged deed
Alienation: 15 Jul 1704 the sum of 6s/4p paid by **Clement Brooke**
Recorded: 21 Aug 1704

• *folio 107a* • Bill of Exchange, 27 Oct 1702
"At 20 days after sight of this my third bill of exchange my first nor second of like tenure and date not being paid pay until **Alexander Magruder** or order the sum of 8£ (value rec'd here) make punctual payment and place it to age as per advice of Your Servant **Splandin Rand**"
To Mr. **John Hide**, merchant in London

• *folio 107a* • Bill of Exchange, 28 Sep 1703
Bill of exchange from **Gabriell Burnam** to pay unto **William Mills** or his order for 17£/3s to **Capt. Timothy Keyfer**, merchant in London

• *folio 107a* • Bill of Exchange, 27 Sep 1703
Bill of exchange from **Samuel Taylor** to **William Mills** for 7£ to Mr. **Joseph Jackson**, merchant in London

---

AUGUST COURT 1704
Att a Prince George's County Court held at Charles Towne the 22nd day of August in the third year of the reign of our Sovereign lady Ann by the Grace of God of England, Scottland, France and Ireland, Queen defender of the faith VIZ her Majesties Justices thereunto authorized and appointed

---

• *folio 108* • Indenture, 17 Apr 1702, in the 14th year of the reign of Lord King William III
From: **Thomas Roper**, bricklayer of Prince George's County
To: **Richard Clarke** of Anne Arundel County, Gent.
For 170£ a 200 acre part of a larger tract called *Roper's Range* lying in Prince George's County between Western Branch and Collington Branch; bounded by land of **Samuel Devall** and **Richard Butts**
Signed: **Tho. Roper** (mark)

25

Witnessed: **Jn'o Price** and **William Taylard**
Memorandum: 17 Apr 1702 **Thomas Roper** acknowledged deed before **Charles Greenberry** and **Amos Garrett**
Alienation: 17 Apr 1702 the sum of 8s paid by **Richard Clarke**
Certification: At the time of the acknowledgement above **Charles Greenberry** and **Amos Garrett** were Justices of the Peace of Ann Arundel County; acknowledged by the Prince George's County Court 18 Sep 1704

• *folio 109* • Indenture, 6 Jul 1703
From: **Richard Clarke** of Anne Arundel County, Gent.
To: **Aaron Rawlins**, planter of Anne Arundel County
    Thomas Roper of Prince George's County by indenture 17 Apr 1702 did convey unto **Richard Clarke** 200 acres of land part of a greater tract called *Roper's Range*; **Richard Clarke** sold this land for 243£ to **Aaron Rawlins**; bounded by land of **Samuel Duvall** and **Richard Butts**
Signed: **Richard Clarke**
Witnessed: **Edward Meriarte** and **Mereen Devall**
Memorandum: 26 Jul 1703 **Elizabeth Clarke** examined by **Richard Jones, Jr.** and **Samuell Chambers**
Alienation: 10 Nov 1703 the sum of 8s for 200 acres paid by **Aaron Rawlings**
Certification: **Richard Jones** and **Samuell Chambers**, Justices of the Peace in Anne Arundel County, acknowledged this deed before **J. Boardley**, Clerk for Anne Arundel County
Recorded: 18 Sep 1704

• *folio 110a* • Appointment of Her Majesties' Clerk, 27 May 1704
From: **Major Wm. Dent**, Attorney General of the Province of Maryland
To: **James Haddock**, Attorney at Law of Prince George's County, Gent.
    Appointment of Haddock to be Clerk of Indictments and prosecutor of Her Majesties cases in Prince George's County
Signed: **William Dent**, Attorney General

• *folio 110a* • Power of Attorney, 10 Apr 1704
From: **Thomas Davy** of London, Mariner
To: **James Haddock**, Attorney at Law
    This document empowers **Atty. Haddock** to act in all circumstances for **Thomas Davy**
Signed: **Thos's Davy**
Witnessed: **Thomas Greenfeild** and **John Wight**

• *folio 111* • Indenture, 15 Jun 1704
From: **Thomas Wall** of Prince George's County
To: **Thomas Gibbins**, planter of Prince George's County
    For 4,900 pounds of good merchantable tobacco a 70 acre parcel of land called *Brookefeild* in Prince George's County on the west side of the Patuxent between the branches of Mattapany Creek and Deep Creek; bounded by **Nath. Truman**
Signed: **Thomas Wall** (mark)
Witnessed: **John Tasker** and **James Stoddart**
Memorandum: 15 Jun 1704 Thomas and his wife **Mary Wall** acknowledged deed before **John Wight** and **James Stoddart**
Alienation: 26 Jul 1704 paid by **Thomas Gibbins**
Recorded: 26 Jul 1704

• *folio 112* • Indenture, 15 Jul 1704
From: **Thomas Gibbins**, planter of Prince George's County
To: **Thomas Wall**, planter of Prince George's County
    For 5,300 pound of tobacco in cask a 50 acre parcel of land called *Smith's Green* lying in Prince George's County and a 50 acre tract called *Smith's Pasture*
Signed: **Thomas Gibbins** (mark)
Witnessed: **John Tasker** and **James Stoddart**

Memorandum: 15 Jun 1704 **Thomas** and **Elizabeth Gibbins** acknowledged deed before **Jno. Wight** and **James Stoddart**
Alienation: 13 Jul 1704 for the sum of 2s paid by **Thomas Wall**

• *folio 113* • Indenture, 25 Nov 1703
From: **Francis Colliar, Sr.** of Prince Georges County, Gent.
To: **John Pottinger, Sr., William Ray, Sr., John Ray, John Turner, Edward Dawson, Solomon Rothery, Robert Harrison, Thomas Lemarr, Sr., John Demall,** and **Archibald Edmundson,** planters of Prince George's County
   Francis Colliar agrees for a 30 to 40 foot tobacco house to be build on the land where he now lives as convenient as possible to Stafford's Cove Landing for the above persons to store their tobacco or goods that might come to the landing for the next 40 years; rent to be one gallon of rum and one capon each paid every year to **Francis Colliar** on the 25th of November
Signed: **Francis Colliar**
Receipt: 25 Nov 1703 received one gallon of Rome (rum) and eleven capons in full for one year's rent, signed **Francis Colliar**
Witnessed: **William Lee** and **Thomas Swaringen**

• *folio 113a* • Agreement, 25 Nov 1703
From: **John Pottinger, Sr., William Ray, Sr., John Ray, John Turner, Edward Dawson, Solomon Rothery, Robert Harrison, Thomas Lemarr, Sr., John Demall,** and **Archibald Edmundson,** planters of Prince George's County
To: **Francis Colliar** of Prince George's County, Gent
   Agreement to conditions of above indenture; no use may be made by anyone except the above named planters or their heirs; if anyone permits storage of other goods a fine of 40s for every hogshead of tobacco will be imposed
Signed by above and witnessed by **William Lee** and **Thomas Swaringen**

• *folio 114* • 12 Year Lease, 4 Nov 1703
From: **Anthony Draine,** planter of Prince George's County
To: **Richard Pile** of Prince George's County, Chrurgion
   For "natural love, good will, and affection" and "other good causes and considerations" give a 9 acre tract of land in Prince George's County, part of a tract called *Something*; bounded by *Brooke Hall*; for rent of one sound ear of Indian corn at time of Nativity
Signed: **Anthony Draine**
Witnessed: **Hugh Ryley, Mary Spell,** and **Thomas Rasberry** (mark)

• *folio 114a* • Indenture, 16 May 1704
From: **Thomas Roper** of Prince George's County
To: **Peregrine Browne,** merchant of London in the Kingdom of England
   For 50£ a tract of 100 acres of *Roper's Chance* and part of a tract of land laid out for Roper for 300 acres warranted to him by **Robert Tyler** of Prince George's County in the freshes near the west side of the Patuxent River; along with 2 servants by the name of **Robert** and **Ann Paine** during the time of their service
Signed: **Thomas Roper** (mark)
Witnessed: **Francis Colliar** and **James Martin**
Factor: **Thomas Wainewright** factor for **Cap. Peregrine Browne**

• *folio 115* • Indenture, 31 Jul 1704
From: **John Lashley,** planter of Prince George's County and **Alce Lashly**
To: **Thomas Wainwright,** merchant of the City of London in the Kingdom of England
   For valuable consideration already paid a 150 acre parcel of land called *Cobreth's Lott* in Prince George's County near the westernmost branch of the said county; bounded by land of **George Plowden,** Collington Run, land of **Christopher Thompson** and the main road
Signed: **John Lashley** (mark) and **Alce Lashley** (mark)
Witnessed: **Robert Bradly** and **John Wight**
Memorandum: 22 Aug 1704 **John Lashly** acknowledged deed before same witnesses

27

Vide ye alienation in folio 123

• *folio 116* • Indenture, 29 Aug 1704
From: **Samuell Taylor**, planter of Prince George's County
To: **Thomas Greenfeild** of Prince George's County
    For 15£ a 150 acre parcel of land called *Taylor's Coast* in Prince George's County on the west side of the Patuxent River in the wood; bounded by land laid out for **Barnard Johnson** called *Doves Pearch*, *Poplar Hills* belonging to **John Boage**, land taken up for **Thomas Kemp**
Signed: **Sam'll Taylor**
Witnessed: **Jn'o Bradford** and **Jn. Lecount**
Memorandum: 29 Aug 1704 **Verlinda Taylor**, wife of Samuel, examined by **Wm. Barton** and **Jno. Wight**
Alienation: 7 Oct 1704 the sum of 6s paid by **Thomas Greenfeild**

SEPTEMBER COURT 1704

Att a Prince George's County Court called and held at Charles Town the 26th day of September 1704 for our Sovereign Lady Ann by the Grace of God Queen of England, Scottland, France and Ireland Defender of the faith and by her Majesties' Justices appointed and authorized (VIZ)
William Barton   John Wightt   Rob't Bradly   William Tanyhill   John Hawkins   James Stoddart

---

• *folio 117* • Indenture, 29 Aug 1704
From: **Nicholas Davis**, planter of Prince George's County
To: **Thomas Greenfeild** of Prince George's County
    For 2,000 pounds of good tobacco a 50 acre parcel of land called *Compass Hills*; bounded by *Poplar Hills*
Signed: **Nicholas Davis**
Witnessed: **Jno. Bradford** and **Jno. Lecomt**
Memorandum: 29 Aug 1704 **Elinor Davis**, wife of Nicholas, examined by **William Barton** and **John Wight**
Alienation: 7 Oct 1704 the sum of 2s paid by **Thomas Greenfeild**

• *folio 118* • Indenture, 28 Sep 1704
From: **Col. Henry Darnall** of Prince George's County, Gent., and **Elinor** his wife
To: **Thomas Brooke** of Prince George's County, Gent.
    For 300 acres of land out of a tract of land belonging to **Thomas Brooke** called *Dann* on Rock Creek in Prince George's County conveyed to his brother **Clement Brook**, Col. Darnall traded a 200 acre parcel of land called *Revertion*, except for a small piece taken away for the lines of **Thomas Sprigg**; bounded by **Thomas Sprigg**, *Beaverdam Branch*, and *Brooke Land*
Signed: **Henry Darnall**
Witnessed: **Henry Hatton, Henry Darnall, Jr., Will. Willinson**
Memorandum: 28 Sept 1704 **Col. Henry Darnall** acknowledged deed before **William Barton** and **R. Bradly**
Alienation: 29 Sep 1704 the sum of 8s paid by **Thomas Brooke**

• *folio 118a* • Indenture 28 Sep 1704
From: **Thomas Brooke** of Prince George's County, Gent., and **Barbara** his wife
To: **Clement Brooke** of Prince George's County, Gent.
    For 200 acres of land called *Prevention* adjoining a parcel of land called *Brooke Grove* which **Thomas Brooke** obtained from **Col. Henry Darnall** for 300 acres of land called *Dann*, **Col. Henry Darnall** and **Thomas Brooke** agreed that the 300 acres of land in folio 118 should be given to **Clement Brooke**
Signed: **Tho. Brooke** and **Barbara Brooke** (mark)
Witnessed: **William Hatton, Hen. Darnall, Jr.** and **Will. Willkeson**
Memorandum: 28 Sep 1704 **Thomas Brooke** and **Barbara**, his wife, acknowledged deed
Alienation: 29 Sep 1704 the sum of 20s paid by **Clement Brooke**

28

• *folio 119a* • Indenture, 22 Aug 1704
From: **Thomas Brooke** of Prince George's County, Esq'r
To: **Robert Owen**, Principle Vestryman of St. Paul's Parish and his associates and brethren the rest of the vestrymen of the said Parish in Prince George's County
    For 8,000 pounds of good sound merchantable tobacco in cask a 120 acre parcel of land called *Brookefeild* in the freshes on the west side of the Patuxent River on a creek called Deep Creek; bounded by land called *The Gears*, *The Plantation*, the road to Mattapany, and Deep Creek. This land was to be used by **Robert Owen** so long as he continue to be minister or curate of the parish and "have the care of soules therein" afterward for the support and maintenance of such other minister according to the Laws of England or the Province...according to the doctrine of the Church of England
Signed: **Tho. Brooke**
Memorandum: 22 Aug 1704 **Thomas Brooke** and **Madam Barbara Brooke** acknowledged the deed before **William Barton** and **John Wight**
Witnesses: **Josiah Willson, Tho. Addison,** and **Ja. Haddock**

• *folio 120a* • Indenture, 30 Mar 1704
From: **Thomas Emmes** of the Kingdom of England, Mariner
To: **Josiah Willson** of Prince George's County
    For 90£ a 250 acre part of a tract of land called *Mt. Calvert Manor* in Prince George's County, formerly Calvert County; bounded by the Patuxent River, land of **Robert Bradly**, land of **Richard Groome**, land of **Christopher Baines**, the main town road, and Groome's Spring Branch
Signed: **Thomas Emms**
Memorandum: Acknowledgement of deed by **Capt. Thomas Emmes** to **Will. Hutchison** and **James Stoddart**

NOVEMBER COURT 1704
Att a Prince George's County Court held at Charles Town the 28th of November 1704 for our Sovereign Lady Ann by the Grace of God Queen of England, Scottland, France and Ireland Defender of the faith and by her Majesties Justices appointed and authorized (VIZ)
Major William Barton   Mr. John White   Mr. Rob't Bradly   Mr. William Tanyhill
Mr. John Hawkins   Mr. Sam'll Magruder   Mr. James Stoddart

• *folio 121a* • Indenture, 24 Jul 1704
From: **John Bowleing** of Charles County and **Mary** his wife
To: **John Winn** of Charles County
    For 7,000 pounds of tobacco a 200 acre tract of land called *The Indian Feild* lying in Prince George's County, formerly Charles County; bounded by Mattawoman Fresh; The *Indian Feild* laid out for 299 acres according to patent is overrun by land called *Hull* belonging to **Stephen Cownrd**?
Signed: **John Bowleing** and **Mary Bowleing**
Witnessed: **Henry Pickett** and **James Hayan**
Endorsement: 24 Jul 1704 **John** and **Mary Bowleing** acknowledged deed before **John Hawkins** and **Robert Wade**

• *folio 122a* • Indenture 14 Oct 1704
From: **Richard Garrell**, planter of Prince George's County and his wife **Alce**
To: **William Scott**, planter of Prince George's County
    "Witnesseth ye said **Richard Isaac**"; "payment of ye said **Richard Jearell**"; for 30£ sold to **William Scott** a 100 acre parcel of land part of a tract called *Denn* lying in Prince George's County near the Eastern Branch of the Potomac River; bounded by land of **Francis Pristley** called *Forgott* and by land of **Col. Ninian Beall**
Signed: **Rich'd Jearell** (mark) and **Alce Jearoll** (mark)
Witnessed: **Samuel Magruder** and **William Tanyhill**
Memorandum: 14 Oct 1704 **Alce Jearell** examined by **William Tanyhill** and **Sam'll Magruder**
Alienation: 2 Dec 1704 the sum of 4s paid by **William Scott**

• *folio 123a* • Indenture, 31 Jul 1703
From: **Jeremiah Macknew**, planter of Prince George's County
To: **Capt. James Bigger**, Gent.
    James Macknew bound himself a servant of "his own free voluntary will" for "good causes and considerations" to **James Bigger** for 5 years "day and night"; **James Bigger** to pay all debts of Macknew and to pay the sheriff's clerk attorney fees, to give Macknew a young horse in 12 months and to supply meat, drink, washing and lodging and necessary apparel
Signed: **Jeremiah Macknew** (mark) and **James Bigger**
Witnessed: **Josiah Willson, James Nuttwell** (mark) and **James Bonifont** (mark)

• *folio 123a* • Indenture, 27 Mar 1704
From: **Thomas Willson**, carpenter of Prince George's County
To: **James Buttler** of Prince George's County
    For 23£/19s/6p a 50 acre parcel of land called *Could Spring Manor* lying on the west side of North Branch of the Patuxent River; **Thomas Willson** bought this land from **Francis Colliar**, Gent.; bounded by land of **Richard Edwards**
Signed: **Thomas Willson** (mark)
Memorandum: 27 Mar 1704 acknowledgement by **Tho. Willson** and **Mary**, his wife before **Robert Tyler** and **Thomas Sprigg**
Payment: 29 Mar 1705 by Bills of Exchange from London, signed **James Butler**
Witnessed: **Robert Tyler** and **Thomas Sprigg, Jr.**
Vide ye discharge of this deed in folio 153

• *folio 114b* • Indenture 20 Dec 1704
From: **James Moor**, planter of Prince George's County
To: **James Stoddart** of Prince George's County, Gent.
    For 85£ a 16 acre parcel of land called *Beall's Guift* in Prince George's County at the dividing branches of the Patuxent beginning at Mount Calvert Point; bounded by *Mount Calvert Manor* and land belonging to **Col. Henry Darnall**
Signed: **James Moore**
Witnessed: **John Wight** and **Robert Bradly**
Memorandum: 2 Dec 1704 (Ed: Indenture dated 20 Dec) **Mary Moor** examined by above witnesses
Alienation: 2 Feb 1704 the sum of 8p paid by **James Stoddart**

• *folio 116b* • Deed of Gift, 20 Dec 1704
From: **Ninian Beall, Sr.** of Prince George's County
To: **Nath'll Taylor**, Minister of Gospel
    For a piece of money called a sixpence "I freely" give a half-acre of land being part of a tract called *The Meddows* on the Western Branch of the Patuxent River in Prince George's County to **Nathaniell Taylor**, to **Robert Bradly, James Stoddart, John Battie, Archibald Edmundson, Thomas Beall, Sr., Thomas Beall, Jr., Ninian Beall, Jr., Charles Beall, Christopher Thompson, Joshua Hall, John Browne, John Henry, James Beall, Alexander Beall, William Ophett, John Soaper** and to their successors
Signed: **Ninian Beall**
Witnessed: **John Wight** and **Sam'll Magruder**

JANUARY COURT 1704
Att a Prince George's County Court called and held the 23rd day of January 1704
for our Sovereign Lady Ann by the Grace of God of England, Scottland, France and Ireland
Queen defender of the faith by Her Majesties Justices thereunto authorized and appointed as VIZ
Robert Bradley Robert Wade John Hawkins Sam'll Magruder James Stoddart: Commissioners

---

• *folio 116c* • Indenture, 8 Nov 1700
From: **Edward Marloe**, planter of Prince George's County, and **Mary** his wife
To: **Terrence Dunning** of Prince George's County

For 2,500 pounds of tobacco and other good causes and considerations a 198 acre tract of half of the land called *Westmoreland* lying in Prince George's County, formerly Charles County, on the south side of the main branch of the Piscattaway; bounded by *Exeter* owned by **John Wheeler**, and the *Manor of Zachia*
Signed: **Edward Marlow** (mark) and **Mary Marlow** (mark)
Witnessed: **Wm. Hutchison** and **Fra. Wheeler**
Endorsement: 8 Nov 1700 acknowledgement of deed and examination of **Mary Marlow** before **Wm. Hutchison** and **John Hawkins**
Memorandum: The conveyance above was delivered to me presently after the same was made over but was mislaid and thought to be lost
Recorded: 25 Feb 1704/5 by **Edward Willett**, Dep'ty Clerk

• *folio 117c* • Indenture, 24 Jan 1704
From: **Thomas Roper**, bricklayer of Anne Arundel County
To: **Thomas Swaringen**, planter of Prince George's County
For 180£ a 100 acre parcel of land called *Swaringen's Enlargement*, part of the 300 acre land called *Roper's Change* which was part of a tract called *Darnall's Grove* in Prince George's County in the freshes on the west side of the Patuxent River; bounded by *Darnall's Grove, Roper's Change*, and land of **Richard Butts**
Signed: **Thomas Roper**
Memorandum: 24 Jan 1704 acknowledged by **Thomas Roper**
Witnessed: **Sam'll Magruder** and **James Stoddart**
Vide ye alienation in folio 136

• *folio 118c* • Six Year Lease, 12 Oct 1702
From: **John Ramsey**, carpenter of Prince George's County
To: **William Linthorne,** planter of Prince George's County
For 500 pounds of bright picked and culled and every way well conditioned leaf tobacco in cask and also for diverse other good causes and valuable considerations *Ramsey's Delight* a 100 acre parcel being part of a larger tract laid out for **John Cousens** called *Lundey*; located on the west side of North Branch of the Patuxent in Prince George's County; a six year lease to William and his wife **Elizabeth Linthorne** for a rent of one capon at 12 o'clock on the Feast of Nativity; they may have one bought servant but no freeman; they may make no waste of timber and shall plant fruit trees; Ramsey may at any time build a house on the property for himself and his daughter; forfeiture 5,000 pounds of tobacco
Signed: **John Ramsey** and **Wm. Linthorne** (mark)
Witnessed: **James Young** and **Nicholas Baker**

• *folio 119b* • Indenture, 26 Jun 1704
From: **Ninian Beall** of Prince George's County, Gent.
To: **Nicholas Rhodes** late of Anne Arundel County
For 60£ the 372 acre plantation called *Beall's Pasture*; bounded by Cattail Marsh
Signed: **Ninian Beall**
Witnessed: **Clement Davis** and **Edward Willett**
Acknowledged in open court
Alienation: 5 Aug 1704 received of **Nicholas Rhodes** the sum of 14s/10p/3f

• *folio 120b* • Indenture, 10 Jan 1704
From: **Thom. Swaringen** of Prince George's County and **Jane** his wife
To: **Charles Hyatt**, planter of Prince George's County
For 66£ a 60 acre parcel of land surveyed and deducted out of a tract called *Basingthorp Hall* now belonging to **Richard Harwood** in the freshes on the west side of the Patuxent River; beginning at a branch of Bears Brooke and bounded by *Basingthorp Hall* and land called *Strife* owned by **Thomas Wells**
Signed: **Thomas Swaringen** and **Jane Swaringen**
Witnessed: **Hugh Riley** and **William Moore** (mark)
Memorandum: 4 Jan 1704 **Jane Swaringen** examined by **Rob. Tyler** and **Tho. Addison**

Alienation: 27 Feb 1704 **Charles Hyatt** paid the sum of 2s

* *folio 121b* • Apprenticeship, 12 Dec 1704
From: **John Bigger,** son of **Cap't James Bigger** of Prince George's County
To: **Thomas Beall, Jr.,** carpenter of Prince George's County
    With the consent of his father **John Bigger** has apprenticed himself to **Thomas Beall, Jr.,** to learn the "science or trade" of carpentering until age 21; John shall not waste the goods of his master at dice or cards or any unlawful game and he shall not go to ordinaries or drinking; at the end of the apprenticeship the master shall give the apprentice a suite of apparel of linen and woolen, shoes, stockings and hat and one set of carpenter tools; during apprenticeship he shall give the apprentice enough schooling so that he can read, write and do accounts
Signed: **John Bigger** (mark) and **Thomas Beall**
Witnessed: **James Stoddart** and **Josiah Willson**

* *folio 121b* • Resurvey, 9 Nov 1704
For: **Luke Gardiner, Jr.,** of St. Mary's County return of a Warrant of the Resurvey of *Frankland* according to ancient meets and bounds expressed in patent
    Josiah Willson, Sheriff of Prince George's County, impaneled and swore the below signed to work with Her Majesties Surveyor
Bounds: Begin at a bounded tree of *Boarman's Content* by oath of **Wm. Hunter, Francis Wheeler** and **Richard Egling** also reputed to be the first bound tree of *Thompson's Rest* now in possessions of **William Hatton** and a second bound tree from a more ancient survey than *Frankland* laid out for **Luke Barbar;** bounded by the west branch of the Piscattaway; **Phillip Lewing's** plantation (Ed: No acreage noted)
Signed: **Josiah Willson, Truman Greenfeild,** Surveyor for Prince George's County, **Richard Conner** (mark), **Rob't Johnson** (mark), **Wm. Hunter** (mark), **Hen. Acton, Henry Guttrich** (mark), **Francis Marbury, J. Leman, Henry Cullver** (mark), **John Miller, Thomas Blandford, Francis Pile** (mark), **John Lenham** (mark)

* *folio 122b* • Resurvey, 24 Oct 1704
For: **James Keech, Jr.,** of St. Mary's County return of a Warrant of the Resurvey of *Locust Thickett* according to ancient meets and bounds expressed in patent
    Josiah Willson, Sheriff of Prince George's County, impanelled and swore the below signed to work with Her Majesties Surveyor
Bounds: Begin at tract called *Thomas His Chance* proved by **George Athey,** land called *Little Ease,* near Piscattaway Branch
Signed: **Josiah Willson, Truman Greenfeild,** Surveyor of Prince George's County, **Christopher Banes, John Rigdon, Thomas Stonestreet** (mark), **Thomas Middleton** (mark), **John Middleton, George Neitor, Jr., William Congley, William Mills** (mark), **Samuel Taylor, Alexander Magruder, Edward Marloe** (mark), and **Nathaniell Magruder** (mark)

* *folio 122c* • Vide ye Conveyance in folio 115:
Alienation: 29 Mar 1705 Mr. **Thomas Wainwright** paid the sum of 3s for 150 acres from **John Lashley**

MARCH COURT 1705
Att a Prince George's County Court held for her most Sacred Majesty
att Charles Towne the 27th day of March 1705 were present
Major Barton   Robert Bradly   Robert Tyler   William Tanihill
Robert Wade   Sam'll Magruder   James Stoddart   Thomas Addison Gent. Justices

---

* *folio 122c* • 20 Aug 1704
From: **Robert Owen,** clerk of Prince George's County
To: **Mr. Willson** and **James Haddock,** Gent. of Prince George's County
    Owen gave **Major Josiah Willson** and **James Haddock** power to act as his attorneys to collect debts owed to him.

Signed: **R. Owen**
Witnessed: **William Barton, Cornelius White,** and **Rich'd Dallam**

• *folio 123b* • Deed of Gift, 18 Sep 1704
From: **Phillip Lewin**, planter of Prince George's County
To: **Edward Jones**, carpenter of Prince George's County
For "natural affection" for my daughter, **Elizabeth Jones**, wife of **Edward Jones**, and her heirs
a 92 acre tract of land called *Phillip's Addition* in Prince George's County, formerly Charles
County; bounded by land formerly laid out for Lewin
Signed: **Phillip Lewin** (mark)
Witnessed: **John Hawkins, Thomas Addison**
Alienation: 20 Jun 1705 the sum of 3s/8p paid by **Edward Jones**

• *folio 123c* • Indenture, 29 Mar 1705
From: **John Murth**, planter of Prince George's County
To: **John Browne**, ship's carpenter of Prince George's County
For 15£ a 100 acre parcel of land called *Wood's Joy* in Prince George's County, formerly
Calvert County, on the west side of the Patuxent River the whole tract of 500 acres originally
surveyed for **Edward Wood**; bounded by **John Anderson**, the river, and land of **Edward Truman**
Signed: **John Murth** (mark)
Witnessed: **James Stoddart** and **William Tanyhill**
Acknowledgement: **John Murth** in front of above witnesses
Alienation: 29 Mar 1705 the sum of 5s paid by **John Browne**

• *folio 124b* • Indenture, 11 Oct 1703 (sic)
From: **Nicholas Sewall** of St. Mary's County , Esq'r
To: **Samuel Pacy**, mariner of the City of London, Kingdom of England
The **Lord Baron of Baltimore** granted to **Thomas Brooke** of Prince George's County a 443 (sic)
acre parcel of land called *Brookefeild* lying in Prince George's County in the freshes on the west
side of the Patuxent River dated 3 Jul 1699; **Nicholas Sewall** purchased 862 acres called *Brookefeild*
from **Thomas Brooke**; for 230£ Sewall sold 443 acres to Pacy; bounded by a parcel called *The
Wedge*, an Indian path near the Indian Fort, and land of **Robert Armes**
Signed: **Nicholas Sewell**, 1705
Memorandum: 11 Oct 1705 **Madame Susana Sewell** examined by **Ken. Cheseldine** and **Jacob
Moreland** regarding sale of this 443 acres
Alienation: 9 Jun 1705 **Joshua Cecell** paid the sum of 9s
Witnesses: **Charles Butler, James Bowley,** and **George Mason**

• *folio 126* • Indenture, 17 Oct 1704
From: **John Ramsey**, carpenter of Prince George's County
To: **John Murdock**, merchant of Prince George's County
For 6,000 pounds of merchantable tobacco a 100 acre parcel of land called *Limidee* from a tract
called *Lundee* given by **John Cousens** to **John Ramsey**
Signed: **John Ramsey**
Endorsement: 11 Oct 1704 **John Ramsey** acknowledged deed before **Robert Tyler** and **Sam'll
Magruder**
Witnessed: **Albert Grumling** and **James Gladston**
Alienation: **John Murdock** paid the sum of 4s

JUNE COURT 1705
Att a Prince George's County Court held for her most Secrett Majesty
att Charles Towne ye 26th day of June 1705
The Worshipfull: Maj. Wm. Barton   Robert Bradly   Robert Tyler   Wm. Tanyhill
Robert Wade Sam'll Magruder   James Stoddart - Gent. Justices

---

- *folio 127a* • Province of Maryland, 20 Jun 1705

"Know all men by these presents that we **Thomas Addison, William Hutchison, John Addison**, Gent. of the County of Prince George's" are firmly bound to Queen Ann 200,000 pounds of good merchantable leaf tobacco and casks for fines and forfeitures and other dues belonging to Her Majesty's government; accounting due by 10th day of April next

Signed: **Thomas Addison, William Hutchison,** and **John Addison**

Witnessed: **William Floyd, Fra. Wheeler, William Jervis,** and **George Noble**

- *folio 127a* • Indenture, 26 Jun 1706

From: **John Mills**, planter of Prince George's County

To: **Nathan Smith**, merchant of Calvert County

For 400 pounds of tobacco a 1 acre and a half and 12 perches; a tract of land being part of a parcel of land lying in the the freshes on the west side of the Patuxent in Prince George's County now in possession of **John Mills**; bounded by land of **Richard Marsham**, the Patuxent River, land of **Clement Hill, Jr.,** Gen'll Surveyor of the western shore the 9th of September 1698

Acknowledged before **Robert Tyler** and **William Tanyhill**

- *folio 128a* • Indenture, 29 Mar 1705

From: **Thomas Larkin** of Anne Arundel County, Gent.

To: **Thomas Pindle** and **Jonathan Simmons,** planters of Prince George's County

For 7£ a 1 acre tract of land bought by **John Larkin** from **Abraham Clarke** called *Essington* on the west side of the Patuxent in Prince George's County; to be held jointly as one parcel of land

Signed: **Thomas Larkin**

Memorandum: 29 Mar 1705 **Margaret Larkin,** wife of Thomas, examined by **Sam'll Magruder** and **Thomas Addison**

Witnessed: **Josiah Willson** and **Christopher Ellis**

Vide ye alienation in folio 166

- *folio 129a* • Indenture, 28 Mar 1705

From: **Clement Hill**, Gent. of Prince George's County and **Ann Hill**

To: **Thomas Swaringen** of Prince George's County

For 130£ a 200 acre tract of land called *Swaringen* formerly called *Hill's Choice*; laid out for **Clement Hill** in the freshes of the Patuxent River in Prince George's County

Signed: **Clement Hill, Jr.** and **Ann Hill**

Witnessed: **James Stoddart** and **Thomas Addison**

Memorandum: 28 Mar 1705 **Ann Hill** examined by above witnesses

- *folio 130* • Indenture, 29 Mar 1705

From: **Robert Tyler** of Prince George's County, Gent.

To: **Matthew Mackebey,** planter of Prince George's County

For 71£ a 104 acre tract of land part of 204 acres called *Tyler's Discovery* in Prince George's County on the west side of the Patuxent River and east side of Collington Branch; bounded by *Enfield Chance* taken up by **John Lewellin** and *Cattail Meadows* owned by **Robert Anderson**

Signed: **Robert Tyler**

Memorandum: **Susanna Tyler,** wife of Robert, gave up her dowry

Alienation: 25 Jun 1705 Matthew Mockabey paid 4s/2p

- *folio 131a* • Indenture, 10 Jan 1704

From: **Charles Hyatt,** cooper of Prince George's County

To: **Hugh Ryley,** carpenter of Prince George's County

For 30£ a tract of 50 acres called *The Beginning,* bounded by *Scott's Lott*, **Thomas Hollyday**'s land called *The Upper Getting* and Collington Branch; located on the west side of the Patuxent River, between the river and Collington Branch.

Signed: **Charles Hyatt**

Witnessed: **Thomas Swaringen** and **William Moore**

Memorandum: 10 Jan 1704 endorsement of **Sarah Hyatt,** wife of Charles

• *folio 132a* • Indenture, 3 May 1705
From: **William Joseph** of Prince George's County, Gent.
To: **John Bradford**, merchant of Prince George's County
For 32£ an 85 acre tract called *Joseph's Good Luck* on the west side of the Patuxent River in the freshes of said river bounded by a tract called *Harris Lott* on the south side of a branch that falleth into Mattapany Creek, and *Essex Lodge*
Signed: **William Joseph**
Memorandum: 19 May 1705 **Elizabeth Joseph**, wife of William, examined by **William Barton** and **James Stoddart**
Witnessed: **James Stoddart, Walter Chira,** and **Clement Brooke**
Alienation: 27 Jun 1705 **John Bradford** paid the sum of 3s/6p

• *folio 133a* • Vide ye deed in folio 115; 2 Feb 1704 **James Stoddart** pays the sum of 8p

• *folio 133a* • Indenture 18 Apr 1705
From: **Josias Towgood** of Anne Arundel County
To: **James Stoddart** of Prince George's County, Gent.
For 13,000 pounds of good sound tobacco in cask a 1 acre tract of *Mount Calvert Manor* located in Prince George's County at the dividing branch on the west side of the Patuxent River, part of a parcel of land called Charles Towne
Signed: **Josias Towgood**
Witnessed: **Rob't Bradly** and **Tho. Addison**
Memorandum: 18 Apr 1705 **Josias Towgood** acknowledged deed before same witnesses

• *folio 134* • Power of Attorney
From: **John Cunningham** of the Kingdom of England
To: **James Stoddart**
John Cunningham, eldest brother's son and heir of **Daniel Cunningham** of Calvert County, for the sum of 27£ and good cause and considerations sold to **William Hutchison** land in Calvert County called *Scott's Lott;* appointed "truly & well beloved friend **James Stoddart**" to act for him
Witnessed: **Samuel Moors, William Stewart, William Tanyhill** and **William Campbell**
Acknowledged: 22 Jun 1705 **William Campbell** came before **Phillip Hoskins** of the Provincial Court
Proved in open court by **William Tanyhill**

• *folio 134a* • Indenture, 1 Jul 1704
From: **John Cunninghame** of the Kingdom of Scotland
To: **William Hutchison** of Prince George's County
For 27£ a 300 acre tract of land called *Scott's Lott* lying in Calvert County; land patented to **Daniel Cunningham** on 1 Aug 1673
Signed: **John Cunningham**
Witnessed: **Samuel Moor, William Tanyhill, William Campbell, William Cunningham,** and **William Stewart**
Great Seal affixed
Acknowledgement: 1 Jul 1704 by **Atty. Burgh**; acknowledged in open court 27 Jun 1705; proved on oath of **Wm. Tanyhill**
Alienation: 19 Jul 1705 the sum of 12s paid by **William Hutchison**

• *folio 135a* • Acknowledgement, 25 Oct 1704
Resurvey of *Locust Thickett*: The jury acknowledged resurvey; bounded by Piscattaway Branch
Vide in folio 122

• *folio 136* • Vide ye conveyance in folio 117; **Thomas Swaringen** paid the sum of 4s for alienation of 100 acres of *Darnall's Grove*

• *folio 136* • Vide ye conveyance in folio 130; **Thomas Swaringen** paid the sum of 8s for alienation of 200 acres of *Hill's Choice*

• *folio 136* • Indenture, 13 _____
From: **Samuell** and **Ann Lyle**
To: **James Bowles**
(Ed: Remainder of page blank. Might this be same as folio 202?)

• *folio 136a* • Indenture, 22 Aug 1702
From: **Nicholas Sewell** of St. Mary's County, Gent., and his wife **Susana**
To: **John** and **William Hollaway**, sons of the late **John Hollaway**, planter of Calvert County, dec'd
For 300£, paid by the father before his death, a 250 acre tract of land called *Partnership* lying on the west side of the Patuxent River in Prince George's County adjoining Collington Branch; bounded by land of **William Raye**
Signed: **Nicholas Sewell** and **Susanna Sewell**
Memorandum: 20 Aug 1704 **Nicholas** and **Susanna Sewell** acknowledged deed before **William Barton** and **John Wight**
Witnessed: **George Therold** and **Clement Brooks**

• *folio 137* • Indenture, 16 Apr 1703
From: **George Jones**, planter of Prince George's County
To: **Isaac Willes** of Prince George's County, Gent.
For 32£ a 100 acre tract of land called *Gedling* adjacent to *Quick Sale* formerly alienated by **Francis Street** to **William Collins** by records of the Calvert County Court; bounded by **Alexander Magruder's** land called *Anchovies Hills* and by *Quick Sale* on the west side of the Patuxent River in Prince George's County
Signed: **George Jones** and **Johanna Jones** (mark)
Witnessed: **Tho. Greenfeild** and **John Wight**
Endorsement: 18 Apr 1703 **Johanna Jones**, wife of George, examined by above witnesses

• *folio 138* • Power of Attorney
From: **Walter Hope** of Blandford in the County of Dorsett, a linen draper
To: **James Stoddart**
For the sum of 40£ those tracts of land called *Hope Yard* and *Hope's Addition* in Prince Georges County bounded in manner specified in the indentures past; **Walter Hope** appoints **James Stoddart** to act as his attorney
Signed: **Walter Hope**
Witnessed: **James Thompson, Robert Johnson** and **William Linney**
Memorandum: Deed recorded in folio 32 of this record and the land sold again by **William Hutchison** to **John Smith** in folio 53 of this records; original deed produced and acknowledged in open court by virtue of the above letter of attorney

• *folio 138a* • Indenture, 24 Sep 1705
From: **Coll. Ninian Beall** of Prince George's County
To: **James Stoddart** of Prince George's County
For 37£ a parcel of land consisting of 2 lots lying in Charles Towne at Mount Calvert in Prince George's County; Royal mines excepted
Signed: **Ninian Beall**
Witnessed: **R. Bradly, John Murdock**, and **Th. Walneior**
Memorandum: 24 Sep 1705 **Ruth Beall**, wife of Ninian, examined by **Rob't Bradly** and **Rob't Tyler**

• *folio 140* • Indenture, 4 May 1705
From: **Coll. Ninian Beall** of Prince George's County, Gent.
To: **William Offeet**, planter of Prince George's County
For 57£/14s/6p a 498 acre parcel of land called *Addition to Caverton Edge* in Prince George's County on the west side of the Patuxent River on the ridge that goes from the Patuxent to the Eastern Branch of the Potomac River
Signed: **Ninian Beall**
Witnessed: **Ro. Bradly** and **James Stoddart**

• *folio 141* • Indenture, 4 May 1705
From: **Ninian Beall, Jr.**, planter of Prince George's County
To: **William Offeet**, planter of Prince George's County
    For 57£/4s/6p a 500 acre parcel of land called *Caverton Edge* lying in Calvert County now Prince George's County on the road that goes to the Eastern Branch of the Potomac River
Signed: **Beall Junior**
Witnessed: **R. Bradly** and **James Stoddart**

• *folio 141* • Indenture, 1 May 1702, the 14th year of the reign of King William III
From: **William Mills** of Prince George's County
To: **Thomas Greenfeild** of Prince George's County
    For a valuable consideration a tract of land called *Dunbarr* in the freshes of the Patuxent River beginning at the ship landing TO HAVE AND TO HOLD until the Feast of St. Michaell next and after for and during 21 years when a fee of 5s is due the heirs of **William Mills** at the "end and expiration of every such one and twenty years to the world's end"
Signed: **William Mills** (mark)
Witnessed: **John Brent** , **Ats. Geive** (mark), **Tho. Truman Greenfeild**
Acknowledgement: 25 Jan 1705 **Tho. Truman Greenfeild** and **John Brent** before **Tho. Brooke**

• *folio 142a* • Indenture, 10 Aug 1705
From: **William Greenup**, planter of Prince George's County
To: **George Smith**, Surgeon of Prince George's County
    For 95£ sold a 100 acre tract of land called *Cumberland*, part of a larger tract called *Cobreth's Lott* in Prince George's County; bounded by Collington Run, Little Branch, *Thorp's Land* or *Beare Garden* owned by **John Browne**
Signed: **Wm. Greenup**
Memorandum: 10 Aug 1705 **Mary Greenup**, wife of William, examined by **Thomas Greenfeild**
Alienation: 14 Aug 1705 **Dr. George Smith** paid the sum of 2s to **Ralph Harryson**
Witnessed: **Truman Greenfeild, Joseph Addison** and **Joshua Cecell**

• *folio 144* • Notification, 26 Aug 1701
From: **James Boog**, merchant in Falkirk in the Kingdom of Scotland
To: **David Lowry**, planter of Maryland
    Ownership of an 800 acre plantation owned by **John Boog** at the time of his death and inherited by his nearest relative, his nephew **James Boog** of Scotland, transferred to **David Lowry** for "a certaine sume of money" and to relieve **James Boog** of all responsibility for any cause relating to his uncle's estate in Maryland.
Signed: **James Boog**, Edinburgh, Scotland
Witnessed: **William Horrey**, merchant, and **Geo. Robertson**, writer

• *folio 144* • Lease, 30 Mar 1704
From: **Nottley Rozer** of Port Tobacco in Charles County, Gent.
To: **Thomas Johnson** of Prince George's County
    For rents and covenants a 200 acre tract of land in Charles County, now Prince George's County called *Green's Purchase* on the east side of Piscattaway River to be run as soon as possible by **Thomas Johnson**; beginning at the Annicostian Fort; for the natural life of **Thomas Johnson, Mary Johnson** his wife, and **Peter Hay** "the longer liver" to pay to **Nottley Rozer** or his heirs a yearly rent of 500 pounds of good sound merchantable tobacco and cask each 10th of December; **Thomas Johnson** shall plant an apple orchard of 200 good apple trees of winter or summer fruits and keep a 27 foot distance
Signed: **Notley Rozer**
Witnessed: **Tho. Addison, Tho. Fletchall**, and **William Thompson**

• *folio 145a* • Indenture, 28 Jan 1705/6
From: **Thomas Greenfeild**, Gent. of Prince's George's County, and **Martha**, his wife
To: **John Rooke**, planter of Prince George's County
    For 2,500 pounds of tobacco a 77 acre tract of land called *Gedling* and part of *Archer's Pasture*;

37

bounded by land of **Mr. Magruder** called *Anchovie Hills*, land of **Isaac Wills**; near the Rouleing Path
Signed: **Tho. Greenfeild**
Memorandum: 28 Jan 1705 **Martha Greenfeild** examined by **Tho. Brooke** and **Frederick Claudius**
Witnessed: **James Haddock** and **Stephen Hoakloy**
Alienation: The sume of 3s/6p

• *folio 146* • Indenture, 25 Nov 1705
From: **William Lee**, planter of Prince George's County and **Ann**, his wife
To: **John Garrard**, merchant of Prince George's County
On 20 Jul 1691 **Francis Collier** and **Sarah**, his wife, of Calvert County made indenture to **Sam'll Griffeth**, planter of Calvert County for the sum of 64£ for a 165 acre tract of land in Calvert County on the west side of the Patuxent River part of *Could Spring Manner*; bounded by land of **Richard Edwards**; 1 Aug 1699 **Samuel Griffeth** and his wife, **Elizabeth**, sold this land for the sum of 12,000 pounds of picked and culled tobacco to **William Lee**; recorded in Prince George's County; **William Lee** and **Ann**, his wife, sold this 165 acres for 155£ to **John Gerrard**
Signed: **William Lee** and **Ann Lee** (mark)
Memorandum: **Ann Lee** examined by **Robert Tyler** and **Abra. Clarke**
Witnesses: **Abra. Clarke** and **Clem't Hill, Jr.**
Alienation: 27 Nov 1705 the sum of 3s/6p paid by **John Garrard** for 165 acres formerly called *Griffith's Purchase*, now called *Flamberts*; rec'd by **Henry Boteler**

• *folio 148a* • Indenture, 22 Dec 1705
From: **John Anderson**, planter of Prince George's County
To: **James Williams**, carpenter of Anne Arundel County
Three indentures of bargain and sale: On 6 Jul 1685 for 100 acres of land part of *Esington*; the second on 13 Jun 1688 for 36 acres part of *Cattaile Meddows*; the third for 20 acres of *Esington* all made between the late **Robert Anderson** of Prince George's County, father of **John Anderson**, and the late **Joseph Williams** of Anne Arundel County, father of **James Williams**; these "shall be cancelled, defaced, and utterly made voyd by these presents" and for "a valuable consideration" paid, **James Williams** will receive a tract of land called *James Lott* part of *Esington* in Prince George's County; bounded by Rouleing Road, near **John Boyd's** road, to **John Boyd's** School, to Cattaile Marsh on the west side of Rouleing Road; to land of **Abraham Clark** called *Esington*; for 156 acres of land
Signed: **John Anderson** (mark)
Memorandum: 22 Dec 1705 **Elizabeth Anderson**, wife of John, examined by **Robert Tyler** and **Abraham Clark**; witnessed by same
Alienation: 22 Jan 1705 the sum of 3s paid by **James Williams**; rec'd by **Henry Boteler**

• *folio 149a* • Quit Claim Deed, 22 Dec 1705
From: **Elizabeth Anderson**, widow of the late **Robert Anderson** of Prince George's County
To: **James Williams**
In consideration of an agreement made between **Robert Anderson** and **James Williams**, son of **Joseph Williams** concerning the sale of 156 acre part of *Esington* to Williams, Elizabeth gives up all rights
Signed: **Elizabeth Anderson** (mark)
Witnessed: **Robert Tyler** and **Abra. Clarke**

• *folio 149a* • Deed of Gift, 19 Oct 1705
From: **Josiah Willson** of Prince George's County, Gent.
To: **Charles Botteler**, son of **Henry Boteler** of Prince George's County, Gent.
"In consideration for the love and affection I bear" and for "other causes and considerations" I "give, grant and confirme" all that 129 acre tract of land called *Willson's Adventures;* bounded by *Harris Lott* belonging to **Henry Botteler** and by land of **Robert Ormes**
Alienation: 26 Nov 1705 **Charles Botteler** paid 5s/3p for the 129 acres
Witnessed: **Tho. Greenfeild**, Justice of the Province

- *folio 150a* • Indenture, 16 Nov 1705
From: **John Gardiner** late of Prince George's County now living in St. Mary's County, Gent.
To: **Luke Gardiner** late of St. Mary's County now in Prince George's County, Gent.
  For 500£ a 12,000 acre tract of land formerly in Charles County now in Prince George's County on the north side of Piscattaway Creek called *Warberton Mannor*; bounded by Piscataway Creek, by "Piscattaway alias Patomack River"
Signed: **John Gardiner**
Witnessed: 16 Nov 1705 **Joshua Guilbert** and **Richard Voules**, two of Her Majesties Justices for St. Mary's County examined **Susanna Gardiner**, wife of **John Gardiner**
Certification: 20 Nov 1703 **Josh. Guilbert** and **Rich'd Voules**, Gent. as Justices of the Peace by **G. Muschamp**, Clerk
Payment: 8 Dec 1705 **John Gardiner** rec'd 500£

- *folio 151a* • Indenture, 5 Dec 1705
From: **James Keech** of St. Mary's County, Gent.
To: **John Smith**, planter of Prince George's County
  For 90£ a parcel of 110 acres taken from a tract of 900 acres called *Thorpland* in Prince George's County near Collington Branch; bound by Perry's Bridge on the road to **Capt. Brock**
Signed: **James Keech**
Memorandum: 5 Dec 1705 deed acknowledge by **Capt. James Keech** and **Elizabeth**, his wife
Witnessed: **R. Bradly** and **James Stoddart**
Alienation: 1 Jan 1705 **John Smith** paid the sum of 5s/6p for 110 acres of *Thorpland*

- *folio 152a* • Vide ye deed in folio 139; 1 Jan 1705 **James Stoddart** paid the sum of one half-penny for alienation of deed

- *folio 152a* • Vide ye deed in folio 90; 18 Nov 1704 **Roger Brooke** paid 5s/3p for alienation of deed

- *folio 152a* • Vide ye deed in folio 114; 1 Oct 1705 received of **Thomas Willson** the sum of 23£/19s/6p which is accepted in full payment for the deed made as security for payment
Signed: **James Butler**
Witnessed: **James Stoddart** and **William Tanyhill**

- *folio 152a* • 15 Year Lease, 18 Sep 1705
From: **William Hutchison** of Prince George's County
To: **William Glover**, carpenter of Prince George's County
  The lower most part of *Sattarday's Work* lying on Jensen's Branch leased for 15 years; Glover not to keep above one freeman at a time for making corn and tobacco; he can cut trees only for use as clapboard or rails except for clearing of ground; he shall plant and tend 150 apple trees; rent will be paid each year of 500 pounds of tobacco; at the end of the lease, he shall leave peaceably
Signed: **Wm. Hutchison** and **William Glover** (mark)
Witnessed: **George Noble** and **Nicholas Devison**
Vide ye endorsement on ye said lease in Liber F in folio 40

- *folio 153* • Indenture, 27 Sep 1705
From: **Thomas Onebee** of Prince George's County
To: **Joshua Cecell** of Prince George's County
  For 12£ a parcel of 42 acres called *Snake* in Prince George's County on the west side of the Patuxent River near the head of Deep Creek; bounded by *Mansfeild*, *The Farme*, *Hargreave* now in possession of **Mrs. Mary Beaven**
Signed: **Thomas Onebee**
Witnessed: **William Selby** and **John White** (mark)
Memorandum: 1 Oct 1705 acknowledgement of deed by **Thomas Onebee**
Witnessed: **Robert Bradly** and **James Stoddart**
Alienation: 6 Oct 1705 **Joshua Cecell** paid the sum of 1s/9p

- *folio 153a* •Indenture, 16 Oct 1705
From: **Clement Brooke** of Prince George's County, Gent
To: **Richard Masham**, planter of Prince George's County
    For 70£ a 240 acre tract of land called *Orphant's Loss*; bounded by *Brooke Groave*, *Brooke's Content*, Jockey Spring Branch, and land already owned by **Richard Marsham**
Signed: **Clement Brooke**
Witnessed: **Edward Willett, Archibald Edmundson,** and **John Warren**
Memorandum: 16 Oct 1705 **Jane Brooke** acknowledged deed in open court
Alienation: 16 Oct 1705 **Richard Marsham** paid the sum of 9s for 240 acres of *Brooke's Content*

Att a Prince George's County Court called and held att Charles Towne ye 26th day of Mar
in the 4th year of the reigne of our Sovereign Lady Ann
by the Grace of God of
England, Scottland, France and Ireland Queen Defender of the Faith 1706 by
her Majesties Commissioners thereunto appoynted and authorized VIZ
Present the Worshippful
Robert Bradly   Robert Tyler   James Stoddart   Will'm Tanyhil

---

- *folio 155* • Indenture, 13 Mar 1704
From: **James Coghill**, planter of Prince George's County
To: **Robert Johnson**, planter of Prince George's County
    For 50£ a 100 acre parcel of land called *Littleworth*; bounded by *Atheis Folly*; lying in Piscattaway Hundred near Broad Creek in Prince George's County
Signed: **James Coghill**
Witnessed: **Rich'd Dallam, Ed'd Botteler,** and **Josh Cecill**
Memorandum: 30 Mar 1704 **Amy Coghill**, wife of James, examined by **John Wight** and **Rob't Bradly**
Alienation: 24 Jul 1704 **Robert Johnson** paid the sum of 4s

- *folio 156* • Indenture, 2 Feb 1705
From: **James Wheeler**, planter of Prince George's County
To: **John Middleton**, planter of Prince George's County
    For 9,000 pounds of tobacco a 200 acre tract called *Wheeler's Purchase* in Prince George's County, formerly Charles County, at the east side of the Piscattaway at an Indian town called Pamunkey; bounded by St. John's Creek, land of **Cap't Luke Gardiner**; this land runs parallel to a patent of 500 acres granted **John Wheeler**, grandfather of **James Wheeler** on 10 Jul 1663; **John Wheeler** willed 200 acres of the land to his brother, **James Wheeler**, now in the possession of **Richard Edgar**, 200 acres willed to above named **James Wheeler** and 100 acres to **Ann Wheeler**, sister of the said James, now wife of **Hillary Ball**
Signed: **James Wheeler** (mark)
Witnessed: **R. Bradly** and **James Stoddart**

- *folio 157* • Letter of Attorney, 1704/5
From: **Thomas Davy**, mariner of the Parish of Reddriff in the County of Surrey
To: **David Greenhill**, mariner of the Parish of St. Mary Wollwick in the County of Kent
    To collect from **James Haddock** in Maryland and all other persons lawful and reasonable debts
Signed: **Tho. Davy**
Witnessed: **Sam'll Norman, Bethell Goodwin**

- *folio 157* • Vide ye conveyance in folio 137; 8 May 1703 **Isaac Wills** paid 4s for alienation of deed

40

By virtue of summons from the Sheriff of Prince George's County **Thomas Addison**, Dep'ty Surveyor, is ordered to lay out and resurvey 3 acres land for a court house and adjoining 2 acres of land for the church in *Charles Towne*

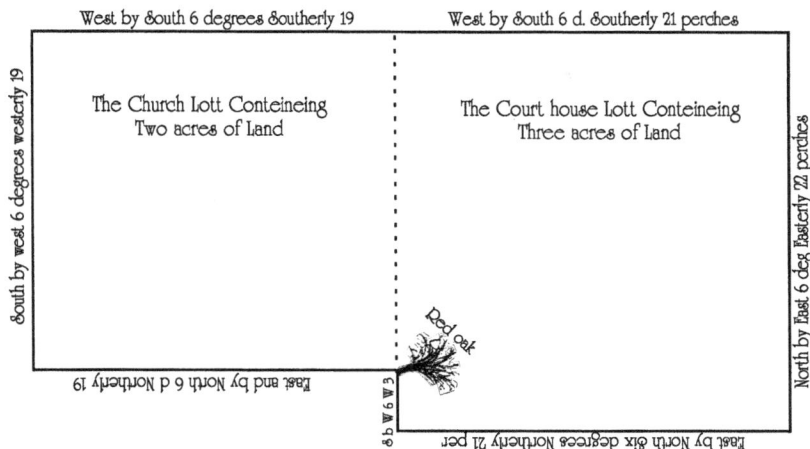

West by South 6 degrees Southerly 19   West by South 6 d. Southerly 21 perches

South by west 6 degrees westerly 19

The Church Lott Conteineing
Two acres of Land

The Court house Lott Conteineing
Three acres of Land

North by East 6 deg Easterly 22 perches

East and by North 6 d Northerly 19

Red oak

W6W3

East by North Six degrees Northerly 21 per

These are therefore humbly to certify that I Thomas Addison, Deputy Surveyor of the afforesaid County have by vertue of ye Order of the Justices afforesaid layd out as followeth first two acres of land for ye use of the Church

Beginning at a bound oak in the towne aforesaid and running then east by north six degrees northerly 19 perches to a poast appointed there to be set according to an Act of Assembly of this province and thence running south by west six degrees westerly ninteen perches to a poast as aforesaid and thence running west and by south 6 degrees southerly to a poast as aforesaid and thence with a straight line to ye first bounded Red Oak containeing and now laid out for two acres of land

By vertue of ye afforesaid order & direction I have allso laid out three acres of land for ye Court house of the said county. Beginning at ye south and last poast of ye aforesaid Church Land and running thence west and by south six degrees southerly twenty one perches to a poast as afforesaid thence north and by east six degrees easterly twenty four perches to a poast as afforesaid thence east by north six degrees northerly twnety one perches to a poast as afforesaid thence south by west six degrees westerly three perches to the first founded Red Oake of the Church Land to ye first poast afforesaid conteining and now laid out for three acres of land this third day of Nov'r 1699

by me Tho. Addison, Dep'ty Surveyor

41

Josiah Willson, Sheriff of Prince George's County commanded by the court to resurvey and laid out a tract of land called *Frankland* for **Luke Gardiner, Jr.**, of St. Mary's County according to the ancient meets and bounds of the patent; the sworn panel of witnesses to the survey: **Francis Marbury, Hickford Leman, Henry Calvert, John Miller, Tho. Blandford, Francis Piles, John Lenham, Richard Conner, Robert Johnson, Wm. Hunter, Henry Acton** and **Henry Guttrick**; bounded by land called *Boarman's Content, Thompson's Rest* now in possession of **William Hatton**, and land of **Luke Barber** (a more ancient survey than that of *Frankland*); on east side of west branch of the Piscattaway; a little below **Phillip Lewin's** plantation; adjoining **Francis Wheeler**

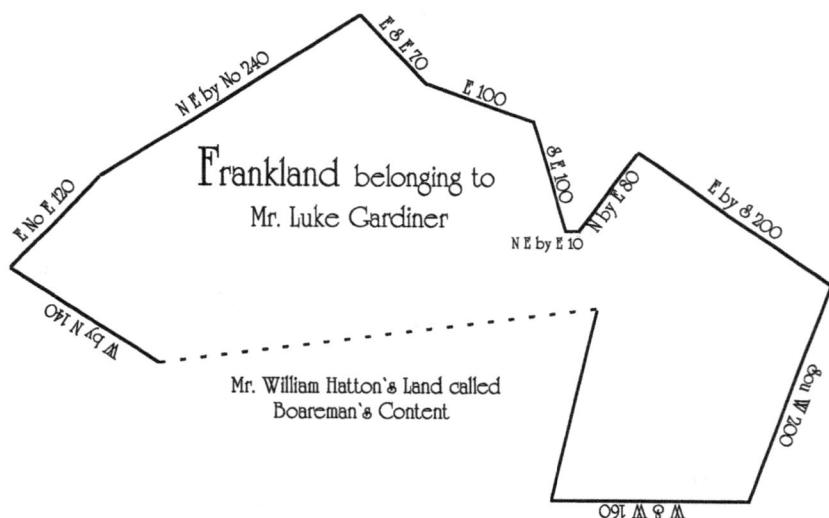

Frankland belonging to
Mr. Luke Gardiner

Mr. William Hatton's Land called
Boareman's Content

Survey platted by Tho. Truman Greenfeild Surveyor Prince George's County

Resurvey of *Scott's Lott* ordered by the Prince George's County Court Clerk; **Col. Ninian Beall** and **James Moore** swore oath of bounded tree; bounded by Collington Branch

Signed: 22 Aug 1705 by **Tho. Addison**, Sheriff, **Clement Hill, Jr., Edw'd Holmes, John Mitchell, Mareen Devall, William Offett, Ishmaell Bateman, Thomas Ricketts, Jr., Nathan Wickam** (mark), **Samuell Brasheer, Morris Miles** (mark), **Solomon Rodery, Benjamin Brasheer**, and **Joseph Browne** (mark)

Surveyed and plotted by **Clement Hill, Jr.**, 22 Aug 1705; examined by **Thomas Addison** 29 Aug 17

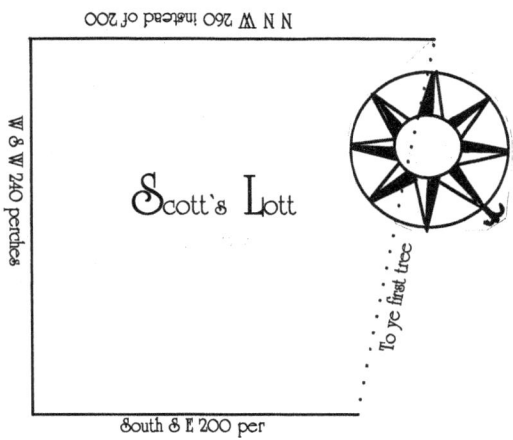

N N W 260 instead of 200

W S W 240 perches

Scott's Lott

To ye first tree

South S E 200 per

• *folio 159* • Return of Survey, 3 Mar 1704/5
The return of the warrant for resurvey of *Locust Thicket* examined by the jury of resurvey
Plotted by a scale of 100 p'r in an Inch by **T. Truman Greenfeild**, Surveyor of Prince George's
County and signed **Thomas Truman Greenfeild**
Examined: 3 Mar 1704/5 and signed **Thomas Addison**

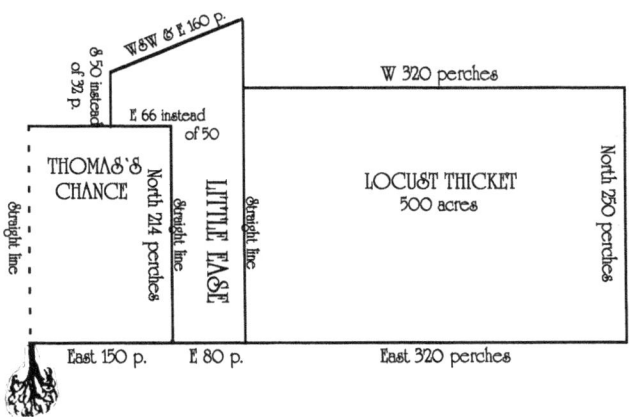

W S W S E 160 p.

S 50 instead of 32 p.

E 66 instead of 50

THOMAS'S CHANCE

North 214 perches

Straight line

LITTLE EASE

Straight line

Straight line

W 320 perches

LOCUST THICKET
500 acres

North 250 perches

East 150 p.

E 80 p.

East 320 perches

43

The jury of resurvey ascertained the bounds of *Kingstone*; beginning at the top of a hill near **Col. Beall's** quarter where **David Small** and **Will Ellis** alias **Shepherd** swore to be the first bound tree

Signed: **Thomas Trueman Greenfeild**

Examined: 16 Mar 1704/5 by **Tho. Addison**

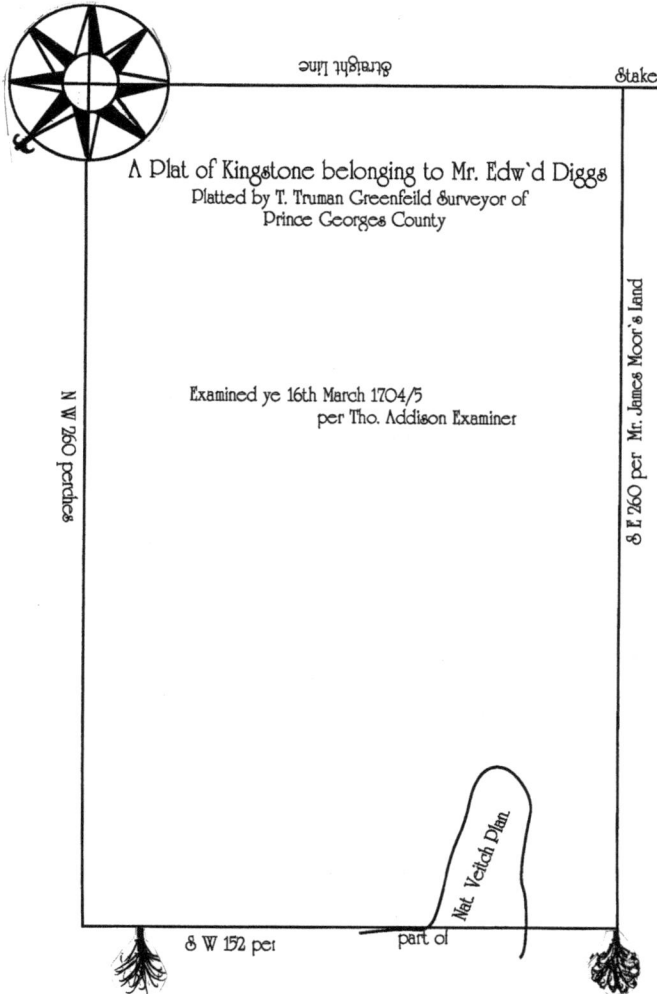

Straight Line   Stake

A Plat of Kingstone belonging to Mr. Edw'd Diggs
Platted by T. Truman Greenfeild Surveyor of
Prince Georges County

Examined ye 16th March 1704/5
per Tho. Addison Examiner

N W 260 perches

S E 260 per Mr. James Moor's land

Nat. Veitch Plan.

S W 152 per   part of

• *folio 160* • Letter of Attorney, 8 Feb 1705
From: **James Rankin**, mariner of London
To: **Hickford Leman** of Maryland
    Rankin appoints Leman to collect money owed to Rankin in the Province of Maryland or Colony of Virginia or to take court action and cast the debtors into prison for non-payment
Signed: **Ja's Rankin**
Witnessed: **William Hutchison** and **Francis Wheeler**

• *folio 160* • Indenture, 23 Feb 1705
From: **John Mills**, planter of Prince George's County
To: **Henry Bottelor** of Prince George's County, Gent.
    For 18£ a 40 acre parcel of land part of a tract laid out for **Thomas Letchworth** on the west side of the north branch of Patuxent River in Prince George's County; bounded by *Fendall's Spring* in possession of **Thomas Willson** and land of **John Taler**
Signed: **John Mills** (mark)
Witnessed: **Henry Rickett** and **James Moulder** (mark)

Att a Prince George's County Court called and held att Charles Towne ye 8th day of June 1706 in the
    fifth year of ye reigne of our Sovereigne Lady Ann Queen of England, Scottland, France, and
    Ireland Defender of the faith & by her Majesties Justices thereunto authorized and appoynted as
        VIZ: Present ye Worshippfull Robert Bradly   James Stoddart   William Tanyhill

---

• *folio 160a* • Indenture, 6 May 1706
From: **Samuell Farmer**, planter of Prince George's County
To: **Robert Wheeler**, carpenter of Prince George's County
    For 70£ a 103 1/4 acre tract of land called *Farmer's Marsh*, part of *Darnall's Grove* in Prince George's County on the west side of Collington Branch
Signed: **Samuell Farmer**
Witnessed: **Robert Tyler** and **Abraham Clarke**
Memorandum: **Elizabeth Farmer**, wife of Samuel, examined by above witnesses
Alienation: 6 May 1706 **Robert Wheeler** paid the sum of 4s

• *folio 162* • Indenture, 6 May 1706
From: **John Baptistyler**, planter of Prince George's County
To: **Samuell Farmer**, planter of Prince George's County
    For 24£ a 50 acre parcel of land called *Farmer's Purchase*, part of a tract called *The Dutchman's Imployment* in Prince George's County; bounded by land of the **Widow Rothery** and land already owned by the said **John Baptistyler**
Signed: **John Baptistyler** (mark)
Memorandum: 16 May 1706 **Ann Baptistyler** examined by **Rob. Tyler** and **Abram Clarke**
Alienation: 20 May 1706 **Samuell Farmer** paid the sum of 2s

• *folio 163* • Indenture, 3 Apr 1706
From: **Luke Gardiner** of Prince George's County, Gent.
To: **John Countee** of Charles County, Gent.
    For 163£/10s a 327 acre tract of land called *Warberton Manner* in Prince George's County, formerly Charles County on the north side of the Piscattaway Creek, part of land called *Comtee's Purchase*; bounded by land of **William Hatton** called *The Ritch Hill, Barbiton's Manner*, and Butler's Cove Branch (Ed: Barbiton and Darberton are possibly the same plantation; the "D" was heavily written over another letter in the first mention of this Manor)
Signed: **Luke Gardiner** and **Ann Gardiner**
Witnessed: **James Stoddart** and **Frederick Claudius**
Memorandum: 3 Apr 1706 **Luke** and **Ann Gardiner** acknowledged deed
Payment: 3 Apr 1706 **John Countee** paid 163£/10s to **Luke Gardiner**

- *folio 163a* • Indenture, 26 Apr 1706
From: **George Plowden** of St. Mary's County, Gent.
To: **Thomas Sprigg** of Prince George's County, Gent.
For 225£ a parcel of "cattle hoggs" and a 480 acre parcel of land being part of *Thorpland* and also part of *Perry Hill*; bounded by Collington Branch in Prince George's County, land of **Major Wm. Barton** bought from Plowden, and land **William Young** bought from Plowden
Signed: **George Plowden**
Memorandum: 26 Apr 1706 **George Plowden** acknowledged deed before **R. Bradly** and **James Stoddart**
Alienation: 24 May 1706 **Thomas Sprigg** paid the sum of 9s

- *folio 165* • Indenture, 28 Jun 1706
From: **Ninian Beall** of Prince George's County, Gent.
To: **Charles Beall** of Prince George's County, son of **Ninian Beall**
For 18£ a 70 acre tract of land called *Lewis Poynt* in Prince George's County; bounded by land of **Christopher Thompson** and Beaver Dam Branch
Signed: **Ninian Beall**
Witnessed: **Henry Botteler** and **Edward Willett**
Acknowledgement: **Ruth Beall** examined by **Edward Willett**, Dep'ty Clerk

- *folio 165a* • Vide ye Deed in folio 129; **Jonathan Simmons & Thomas Pindle** paid the sum of 6p

- *folio 165a* • Indenture, 10 Aug 1704
From: **Mordicay Moore**, merchant of Anne Arundel County
To: **Charles Burges** of Anne Arundel County, Gent.
The late **George Yale** and **Mary** his wife of Anne Arundel County on 23 Nov 1687 sold the 500 acre tract called *Westfelia* to the Widow **Ursula Burges**, since wife of **Mordecay Moore**, now deceased; *Westfelia* then lying in Calvert County and now Prince George's on the west side of the main branch of the dividing creek of the Patuxent River; bounded by land laid out for **Benjamin Wells** called the *Vale of Benjamin*; 17 Nov 1700 **Ursula Burges Moore** willed the land to her husband **Mordicay Moore** to dispose of in whatever manner he wished; sold to **Charles Burges**, the natural son of Ursula
Signed: **Mord'a Moore**
Witnessed: **Th. Jones** and **John Beale**
Endorsement: **Dr. Mordecay Moore** acknowledged deed before **Samuel Young** and **John Hill**

- *folio 166a* • Indenture, 5 Sep 1705
From: **William Joseph, Junior**, of Prince George's County given power of attorney by his father, **William Joseph, Esq'r**, late of Prince George's County
To: **James Butler**, planter of Prince George's County
For 500£ two parcels of land; one called *Hermitage* in Prince George's County on the east side of the main branch that falls in the Potomac and the other called *Joseph's Park*; *Hermitage* of 3,866 acres from 2 warrants, one for 2,000 acres and the other for 1,689 acres both granted 17 Apr 1689; total 4,220 acres
Signed: **William Joseph**
Witnessed: **James Stoddart**, **William Tanyhill**, and **Tho. Macnemarra**
Endorsement: 18 Oct 1705 by **James Butler** before **James Stoddart** and **William Tanyhill**, commissioners for Prince George's County
Alienation: 17 Nov 1705 **James Buttler** paid the sum of 7£/14s/8p

- *folio 167a* • 14 Nov 1702
From: **David Lowry**, planter of Prince George's County
To: **William Wattson**, planter of Prince George's County
The sum of 10,000 pounds of good sound merchantable tobacco and cask to be paid **William Wattson**; now **David Lowry** has sold **William Wattson** part of a tract called *Poplar Hill* formerly surveyed for **John Boage** of Maryland, deceased; lying in Prince George's County in the branches of Aquasco Creek on the Patuxent River; bounded by **William Mills**, the south corner of the

"Chapple"; **William Wattson** bound himself to pay 2,000 pounds of picked and culled tobacco for each 100 acres of land
Signed: **David Lowry** (mark)
Witnessed: **Tho. Greenfeild, T. Truman Greenfeild, James Wapple** (mark)

• *folio 168* • Indenture, 15 Jul 1706
From: **John Mills**, planter of Prince George's County
To: **Charles Walker**, planter of Prince George's County
    For 11£/17s/6p a 50 acre parcel of land in the woods of the uppermost part of a tract of 150 acres laid out for **Thomas Letchwith** and sold to **John Tale**, deceased; conveyed from Tale's son to **John Milles**; lying on the west side of the Patuxent River in the North Branch in Prince George's County; bounded by land called *Mount Pleasant*
Signed: **John Mills**
Witnessed: **Rob't Tyler** and **Henry Mace**

• *folio 169* • Indenture, 12 Jul 1706
From: **Robert Brooke**, planter of Calvert County
To: **John Smith**, planter of Prince George's County
    For 150£ a 225 acre tract of land part of a larger tract called *Freindshipp* formerly *Brookewood* in Prince George's County; bounded by land of **Baker Brooke**
Signed: **Rob't Brooke**
Memorandum: 12 Jul 1706 **Robert** and **Grace Brooke** ack'd deed before **Jn. Mackall** and **Tho. Hero**
Witnessed: **John Boon** and **Benj. Mackall**
Alienation: 18 Jul 1706 **John Smith** paid the sum of 4s and a sixpence to **Henry Botteler**

• *folio 170* • Commission of the Peace, 20 Apr 1706
From: **Governor John Seymour** for Queen Anne
To: **Robert Bradly, Robert Tyler, James Stoddart, William Tanyhill, John Garrard, Frederick Claudius, Abraham Clark, Thomas Brooke, Jr., Francis Marlbrough, Thomas Cleggett, Alexander Magruder** and **Henry Acton** of Prince George's County
    Appointed Justices to keep the peace within the County of Prince George's according to the laws of the Kingdom of England; to hand out punishment and hold in custody those who misbehave; **Robert Bradly, Robert Tyler, James Stoddart** and **William Tanyhill** appointed Justices to inquire into witchcraft, enchantments, sorcerer's art, magic, etc.; investigate any abuse of weights and measures or in selling of any liquors not according to the form, force and effect of the Acts of Assembly for the common good; "afforesaid witness our trusty and well beloved **John Seymour**, Esq'r Cap. Generall and Governour in Chiefe of our said Province att ye towne and poart of Annapolis the 20th day of Aprill"
Signed: **John Seymour**

• *folio 170a* • 18 Apr 1706
From: **Governor John Seymour** for Queen Anne
To: **William Tanyhill, John Garrard** and **Frederick Caludius** of Prince George's County
    Authorization to administer oaths appointed by the Act of Parliament to be "admin'd instead of the Oaths of Allegance and Supremecy the Oath of Abjuration and the accustomed Oath of Justice to **Robert Bradly, Robert Tyler** and **James Stoddart**"
Signed: **John Seymoure**

• *folio 170a* • Commission of the Peace, 18 Apr 1706
From: **Governor John Seymour** for Queen Anne
To: **Robert Bradly, Robert Tyler, James Stoddart, William Tanyhill, John Garrard** and **Frederick Claudius** of Prince George's County
    "Any three of you" to judge any persons offending against any ordinance or statute called before you: Those who threaten to do bodily harm to any of our good people or to burn their houses or otherwise break our peace...shall be committed in safe custody...to act wherein the demand does not exceed 10,000 pounds of tobacco and 50£....
Signed: **Jo. Seymour**

From: **Governor Seymour**

To: **William Tanyhill, John Garrard,** and **Frederick Claudius** of Prince George's County

Authorization to administer Oath of Justice to **Robert Bradly, Robert Tyler** and **James Stoddart** and certify the same "to us in our High Court of Chancery"

Signed: **Jo. Seymour**

• *folio 171b* • Survey Map of division of *Major's Lott*

From: **Col. Beall**

To: **John Pottinger**

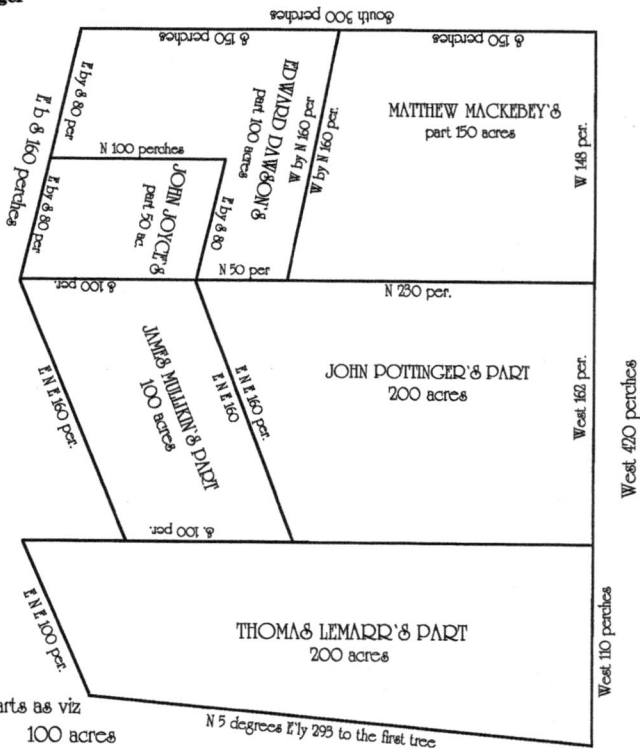

The Several Parts as viz

James Mullikin	100 acres
John Joyce	50
Edward Dawson	100
John Pottinger	200
Thomas Lemar	200
Mathew Mackbey	150
	800

The above is the severall parts of the Major's Lott w'ch by Pattent containes 800 acres and is divided as above by W'm Hutchsion Sur'r

48

- *folio 171b* • **Robert Middleton, Senior**, desires to have his mark recorded as VIZ: A swallow fork and hole in each ear both hogs and cattle

- *folio 171b* • **James Middleton** desires to have his mark recorded as VIZ: A swallow fork and hole in the right ear and a crap and over bitt and an under bitt on the left, both cattle and hogs

- *folio 171a* #2 • Indenture, 8 Feb 1704
From: **Ann Walker** of Prince George's County
To: **Cap't George Harris**, merchant of Prince George's County
Ann being the only daughter and heir at law of the late **William Rought** of Calvert County for 10£ for a 10 acre tract of land called *Twiver* on the west of side of the Patuxent River formerly in Calvert now in Prince George's County; bounded by the Patuxent River
Signed: **Ann Walker** (mark)
Witnessed: **Mary Cecill** (mark), **Rice Owen** (mark) and **Josh'a Cecell**
Memorandum: **Ann Walker** examined 26 Feb 1704 by **Robert Bradly** and **James Stoddart**

- *folio 172a* • Indenture, 20 Nov 1705
From: **Samuell** and **Verlinda Taylor** of Charles County
To: **William Hutchison**, merchant of Prince George's County
Verlinda Taylor, one of the 6 children of the late **Robert Doyne** of Charles County, Gentleman, inherited 181 acres called *Carrick Fergus* granted **Robert Doyne** by the Right Honorable Charles, Lord and Proprietor of Maryland dated 5 Apr 1684; located in Piscattaway in Charles County, now Prince George's County; bounded by *Friendship* owned by **Mr. Wade** and *Vainall* owned by **Mr. Fooker**, to Kosconco Creek, and land of **Randolf Hinson**; children of **Robert Doyne** were **Wharton Doyne, William Doyne, Sarah, Verlinda, Elinor** and **Mary Doyne**
Memorandum: 20 Nov 1705 **Verlinda Taylor** examined by **Frederick Claudius** and **William Tanyhill**
Signed: **Sam'll Taylor** and **Verlinda Taylor**
Alienation: **Wm. Hutchison** paid the sump of 4s

Ann by the Grace of God of England, Scottland, France and Ireland Queen Defender of the faith att a Court called and held att Charles Towne for her said Majesty Queen Ann the 25th day of Aug 1706 by her Majesties Justices thereunto authorized and appoynted   Present the Worshipfull
Robert Bradly   Rob't Tyler   James Stoddart   John Garrard   Frederick Claudius

---

- *folio 174* • Letter of Attorney, 4 Aug 1706
From: **James Wallace**, merchant late of London in the Kingdom of England now of Prince George's County
To: **Andrew Hambleton**
Hambleton appointed to handle all debt collection of **James Wallace** in Maryland
Signed: **Ja. Wallace**
Witnessed: **David Small** and **James Riggs**

Att a Prince George's County Court held att Charles Towne on ye 8th day of September 1706 for her Majesty Queen Ann of England, Scottland, France and Ireland Defender of the faith
By her Majesties Justices thereunto authorized and appoynted   (Ed: No names listed)

- *folio 174* • Indenture, 4 Feb 1705
From: **Joshua Hall**, planter of Prince George's County
To: **Clement Hill** of Prince George's County, Gent.
For 105£ 3 parcels of land in Prince George's County on the west side of the North Branch of the Patuxent River VIZ: One 70 acre tract called *Joyants Rainge (Giant's Range)* part of a tract called *Pentlin Hills*, bounded by 30 acres **Joshua Hall** reserved for himself; another tract of 101 acres called *The Range* bounded by Collington; a third tract of 50 acres called *New Castle* bounded by *Giant's Range* near Mt. Pleasant Path and land of **Mr. Tasker**

49

Signed: **Joshua Hall**
Witnessed: **James Stoddart** and **John Frogg**
Acknowledgement: 29 Jun 1706 **Joshua Hall** and **Margrett,** his wife acknowledged deed before **R. Bradly** and **James Stoddart**
Alienation: 24 Sep 1706 **Clement Hill, Jr.,** paid the sum of 9s

---

Att a Prince George's County Court called and held att Charles Towne ye 27th day of November 1706 for our Sovereigne Lady Ann by the Grace of God of England, Scottland, France and Ireland Queen Defender of the faith by her Majesty's Justices thereunto authorized and appoynted
Present ye Worshipfull   Robert Bradly   Robert Tyler   James Stoddart
William Tanyhill   John Garrard   Frederick Claudius

• *folio 175a* • Deed of Gift, 2 Oct 1706
From: **John Pigman,** cooper of Prince George's County
To: **Anthony Long,** planter of Prince George's County
   John Pigman lived on a tract of land called *Tannton* of 137 acres; he gave 37 acres to **Anthony Long**
Signed: **John Pigman**
Witnessed: **Henry Acton**

• *folio 175a* • Indenture, 21 Nov 1706
From: **Hillary Ball,** Planter of Prince George's County and **Ann,** his wife
To: **William Hutchison** of Prince George's County
   For 3,000 pounds of tobacco a 100 acre parcel of land in Prince George's County, formerly Charles County; part of a tract of land called *Wheeler's Purchase* surveyed by **John Wheeler,** dec'd, and left to **John, James** and **Ann Wheeler; Ann** being the wife of **Hillary Ball;** bounded by **James Wheeler** and the Potomac River
Signed: **Hillary Ball** and **Ann Ball** (mark)
Witnessed: **Francis Marbury** and **Henry Acton**
Memorandum: **Ann Ball** examined by **Coram Nobn, Francis Marbury** and **Henry Acton**
Alienation: 27 Nov 1706 **William Hutchison** paid the sum of 2s

• *folio 176* • Indenture, 20 Nov 1706
From: **John Middleton,** planter of Prince George's County
To: **William Hutchison** of Prince George's County, Gent.
   For 40£ a 200 acre parcel of land lying in Prince George's County, formerly Charles County; part of tract called *Wheeler's Purchase* surveyed for **John Wheeler** and sold by **James Wheeler** to **John Middleton;** bounded by **John Wheeler's** part now in possession of **Richard Edgar**
Signed: **John Middleton** and **Mary Middleton** (mark)
Witnessed: **Francis Marbury** and **Henry Acton**
Memorandum: 21 Nov 1706 **Mary Middleton** examined by above witnesses
Alienation: 27 Nov 1706 **William Hutchison** paid the sum of 4s

---

Att a Prince George's County Court held att Charles Towne the 2nd day of January 1706 in the fifth year of the Reigne of our Sovereigne Lady Ann by the Grace of God of England, Scottland, France and Ireland Queene Defender of the faith by her Majesties Justices thereunto authorized and appoynted as VIZ
Present the Worshippful   Robert Bradly   Robert Tyler   William Tannyhill   James Stoddart

---

• *folio 178* • Indenture, 2 Jan 1706
From: **Phillip Lynes** of Charles County, Gent., and his wife **Ann**
To: **William Harbert** of Charles County, Gent.
   The Right Honorable Cecillius, Lord Baron of Baltimore granted at the City of St. Mary's on 22 Sep 1665 unto **John Clarke** a tract of land called *Clarke's Inheritance* lying in Charles County on

the north side of the main fresh run at the head of Mattawoman & Thomas's Creek; commonly known as *Nattingee* containing 500 acres; 9 Jan 1681 **John Clarke** signed over this original grant to his brother, **Thomas Clarke**; 10 Jan 1681 **Thomas Clark** in open Court in Charles County sold the land to **John Godshall** of Charles County; 8 Jun 1683 **John Godshall** sold the land to **Phillip Lynes** recorded in Charles County records; for 120£ **Phillip** and **Ann Lynes** now sell the 500 acres of *Clarke's Inheritance* now lying in Prince George's County
Signed: **Phillip Lynes**
Witnessed: **John Connlee** and **Charles James**
Memorandum: 2 Jan 1706/7 **Ann Lynes** examined in Charles County by above witnesses
Certification: The two mentioned gentlemen subscribers to this endorsement on this deed are two of her Majesties Justices of Charles County; signed by **E. Howard**, Clerk
Vide ye alienation in folio 226

- *folio 179a* • Indenture, 20 Aug 1706
From: **John Giles**, planter of Anne Arundel County
To: **James Beall**, planter of Prince George's County
    For 100£ a one quarter part or 222 acres of *Good Luck* formerly granted **Zachiriah Wade** and **Luke Gardiner**; **Luke Gardiner, Jr.** sold to **John Giles**
Signed: **John Giles**
Witnessed: **Rob't Bradly, John Wall** and **James Stoddart**
Memorandum: 25 Sep 1706 **John Giles** and **Sarah** his wife acknowledged this deed before **R. Bradly** and **James Stoddart**
Alienation: 29 Jan 1706/7 **James Beall** paid the sum of 4s signed **Ralph Harrison**

- *folio 180* • Indenture, 9 Oct 1706
From: **Clement Hill** of Prince George's County, Gent.
To: **Joseph Willson**, planter of Calvert County
    For 111£ a 269 acre parcel of land part of a tract called *Baltimore* laid out for 1,000 acres in Prince George's County; beginning at the mouth of a small branch that issues out of Beaverdam Branch; **Ann Hill**, wife of **Clement**, examined by **James Stoddart** and **J. Gerrard** and witnessed by same

Att a Prince George's County Court held att Charles Towne ye 25th day of March in the sixth year of the Reigne of our Sovereigne Lady Ann by the Grace of God of England, Scotland, France and Ireland Queen Defender of ye faith by her Majesties Justices thereunto authorized and appoynted Present the Worshipfull Robert Bradly William Tanihill Frederick Claudius Thomas Cleggett

- *folio 181* • Deed of Gift, 24 Mar 1706
From: **John Browne, Senior**, planter of Prince George's County
To: **John Browne, Junior**
    John Browne, Jr., "becomes bound with his father to **Peter Paggon** and Company, Merchants in London for securing the payment of certain sum of money and tobacco" which **John Browne** the Elder owes; for this and "natural love and affection" John, the Elder, then gives his son a parcel of land called *Warmaster*
Signed: **John Browne**
Witnessed upon delivery of 6p: **Francis Colliar**

- *folio 181a* • 15 year Lease, 18 Sep 1705
From: **William Hutchison** of Prince George's County
To: **William Glover**, carpenter of Prince George's County
    The lowermost part of land called *Satterdayes Worke* lying on Jenson's Branch leased to **William Glover** who may not keep more than one free man at a time to plant corn or tobacco; no timber may be cut except for clap boards or rails for fences or clearing of ground; he shall plant, prune and tend 150 apple trees
Signed: **Wm. Hutchison** and **William Glover** (mark)
Witnessed: **George Noble** and **Nicholas Fenown**

51

• *folio 181a* • Letter of Attorney, 25 Sep 1706
From: **Hugh Graham**, Chururgion (Surgeon) of the City of Philadelphia in the Province of Pennsylvania
To: **James Haddock** of Potomac in the Province of Maryland, Gent.
    Appointment of **James Haddock** to collect debts in the Province of Maryland for **Dr. Graham**
Signed: **Hugh Graham**
Witnessed: **Richard Jones, Jr.**, and **Tho. Gassaway**

• *folio 182* • Letter of Attorney, 25 Sep 1706
From: **John Vanlawr**, merchant of Philadelphia
To: **James Haddock** of Prince George's County, Gent.
    Appointment of his "trusty and well beloved friend" to collect his debts in Maryland
Signed: **John Vanlawr**
Witnessed: **Richard Jones, Jr.** and **Tho. Gassaway**

• *folio 182* • Letter of Attorney, 16 Sep 1706
From: **John Frogg** of Philadelphia in the Province of Pennsylvania
To: **James Haddock** of Prince George's County in the Province of Maryland
    Haddock appointed to collect debts in Maryland
Signed: **John Frogg**
Witnessed: **Wm. Hutchison** and **John Warren**

• folio 182a • Indenture 28 Jun 1706
From: **Thomas Wintersell**, planter of Anne Arundel County
To: **John Brice**, merchant of Anne Arundel County
    For 10£ a 400 parcel from a tract of land called *Wintersell's Range* in Prince George's County taken up 25 Jul 1703 by virtue of a warrant granted to **Henry Roper, Thomas Roper** and **Thomas Wintersell** dated 11 Jan 1702 for 1,200 acres and by his Lordship's patent dated 10 Nov 1703; bounded by *William's Range*, by the main branch of the Piency Branch of the Eastern branch of the Potomac and by *Bacon Hall*
Signed: **Thomas Wintersell**
Witnessed: **Lenard Wayman** and **Martha Devall**
Memorandum: 28 Jun 1706 **Thomas Wintersell** and his unnamed wife acknowledged deed before **Lewis Devall** and **Tho. Larkin**
Alienation: 13 Aug 1706 **John Brice** paid the sum of 16s
Certification: Deed acknowledged by **Lewis Devall** and **Thomas Larkin** of Anne Arundel County, Gent. 26 Jul 1706 before **Tho. Bordly**, Clerk of Anne Arundel County

• *folio 183a* • Indenture, 24 Feb 1706
From: **Thomas Ricketts**, planter of Anne Arundel County
To: **Thomas Fowler**, planter of Prince George's County
    For 120£ a 300 acre part of a tract of 463 acres called *Ridgly's and Tyler's Chance* in Prince George's County; bounded by *Willson's Plaines* in possession of **Mareen Devall, Jr.**, it being the NW corner of land laid out for **Lewis Devall** also part of *Ridgly's and Tyler's Chance*
Signed: **Thomas Ricketts**
Memorandum: 20 Feb 1706 **Sarah Ricketts** examined by **Rob't Tyler** and **J. Gerard**
Vide ye alienation folio 202

• *folio 184a* • Obligation, 30 May 1704
From: **William Hutchison** of Prince George's County
To: **John Addison** of Prince George's County
    The sum of 500£ to be paid on demand by **Wm. Hutchison**; condition of obligation involves a partnership between the two men involving several parcels of land including *Strife* estimate about 800 acres, *Freindshipp* of 856 acres, a tract called *White Heaven* of 759 acres and a tract called *Carlile* of 146 acres; at the death of one the land falls to the survivor
Signed: **Wm. Hutchison**
Witnessed: **Ja. Wallace** and **Francis Wheeler**

- *folio 184a* • 7 Jan 1705
From: **Edward** and **Arther Turner**
To: **Thomas Addison** of Prince George's County
    Addison is empowered to take possession of a plantation called *Batchelor's Harbor* and dispossess **Gilbert Marsh**
Signed: **Edward Turner** and **Arther Turner** (mark)
Witnessed: **Tho. Hobb** and **Wm. Hobb**
Acknowledgement: 4 Jan 1705/6 **William Hobb** made oath that the above signatures were witnessed by him, sworn before **John Addison**

- *folio 185* • 15 year Lease, 26 Oct 1705
From: **Rich'd Wade** of Charles County, Gent
To: **Dan'll Delozer**, tailer of Charles County
    For diverse good causes and considerations a 100 acre tract of land in Prince George's County called *Wade's Adventure*; one ear of Indian corn to be paid each December 25; to plant an orchard of 200 trees
Signed: **Rich'd Wade** and **Dan'll Delozer** (mark)
Witnessed: **John Slellen** and **Archibald Bishop**
Acknowledgement: 29 Aug 1706 **Richard Wade** and **Daniell Delozer** came before **Tho. Dent** and **Rich'd Harrison**

- *folio 185a* • Deed of Gift, 10 Mar 1706
From: **Ninian** and **Ruth Beall** of Prince George's County
To: **Charles Beall**, son
    Of one Negro girl called **Doll** about eight years of age
Signed: **Ninian Beall** and **Ruth Beall** (mark)
Witnessed: **Thomas Evans** and **Alex'r Ross** (mark)

- *folio 185a* • Deed of Gift, 10 Mar 1706
From: **Ninian** and **Ruth Beall** of Prince George's County
To: **Ninian Beall, Jr.**, son
    Of one Negro girl called **Pegg** about 4 years of age
Signed: **Ninian Beall** and **Ruth Beall** (mark)
Witnessed: **Thomas Evans** and **Alex'r Ross** (mark)

- *folio 185a* • Deed of Gift, 10 Mar 1706
From: **Ninian** and **Ruth Beall** of Prince George's County
To: **Thomas Beall**, son
    Of one Negro boy called **James** about 10 years of age
Signed: **Ninian Beall** and **Ruth Beall** (mark)
Witnessed: **Thomas Evans** and **Alex'r Ross** (mark)

- *folio 186* • Deed of Gift, 10 Mar 1706
From: **Ninian** and **Ruth Beall** of Prince George's County
To: **John Beall**, son
    Of one Negro girl called **Rose** about 4 years of age
Signed: **Ninian Beall** and **Ruth Beall** (mark)
Witnessed: **Thomas Evans** and **Alex'r Ross** (mark)

- *folio 186* • Deed of Gift, 10 Mar 1706
From: **Ninian** and **Ruth Beall** of Prince George's County
To: **George Beall**, son
    Of one Negro boy called **Will** of seven years of age
Signed: **Ninian Beall** and **Ruth Beall** (mark)
Witnessed: **Thomas Evans** and **Alex'r Ross** (mark)

• *folio 186* • Deed of Gift, 10 Mar 1706
From: **Ninian** and **Ruth Beall** of Prince George's County
To: **Hester Beall**, daughter, wife of **Joseph Belt** of Prince George's County
    Of a Negro girl about 12 years of age
Signed: **Ninian Beall** and **Ruth Beall** (mark)
Witnessed: **Thomas Evans** and **Alex'r Ross** (mark)

• *folio 186a* • Deed of Gift, 10 Mar 1706
From: **Ninian** and **Ruth Beall** of Prince George's County
To: **Mary Beall**, daughter
    Of a Negro girl about 5 years of age called **Nanny**
Signed: **Ninian Beall** and **Ruth Beall** (mark)
Witnessed: **Thomas Evans** and **Alex'r Ross** (mark)

• *folio 186a* • Deed of Gift, 10 Mar 1706
From: **Ninian** and **Ruth Beall** of Prince George's County
To: **Rachell Beall**, daughter
    Of a Negro girl called **Betty** about 11 years of age
Signed: **Ninian Beall** and **Ruth Beall** (mark)
Witnessed: **Thomas Evans** and **Alex'r Ross** (mark)

Att a Prince George's County Court called & held att Charles Towne ye 26th day of August in the Sixth yeare of the Reign of our Sovereigne Lady Ann by the grace of God of England, Scottland, France and Ireland Queen & by her Majesties Justices thereunto authorized & appointed as VIZ
    Present ye Worshipfull   Robert Bradly   Robert Tyler   William Tannyhill   John Gerrard
          Frederick Claudius   Tho. Clegget   Allex. Magruder   Henry Acton

---

• *folio 187* • 19 Jul 1707
From: **Rebecca Addison**, Senior Relict of the **Honorable John Addison** late of Prince George's County, Deceased
To: **Thomas Addison**
    For the sum of 620£ to be paid by **Thomas Addison**, son and heir of **John Addison**, **Rebecca Addison** gives up all her rights to the any part of the estate of **John Addison, Esq'r**
Signed: **Rebecca Addison** (mark)
Acknowledgement: 19 Jul 1707 **Thomas Addison** paid the 620£ signed by **Rebecca Addison**
Witnessed: **H. Leman, William Hutchison, Ja. Haddock, John Mitchell, John Warren**
Proved in open court by the testimony of **Hickford Leman** and **John Mitchell**

• *folio 187a* • 19 Jul 1707
From: **Thomas Addison** of Prince George's County, Gent.
To: **Rebecca Addison**, widow of Prince George's County
    Thomas Addison binds himself and his heirs to pay **Rebecca Addison** 300£ on the 20th of July 1709; money to be paid by Bills of Exchange but only "by an order on some merchant in England"
Signed: **Thomas Addison**
Witnessed: **Wm. Hutchison, Ja. Haddock,** and **H. Leman**
Proved in open court by the testimony of **Ja. Haddock** and **H. Leman**

• *folio 187a* • 19 Jul 1707
From: **Thomas Addison** of Prince George's County, Gent.
To: **Rebecca Addison** of Prince George's County
    Thomas Addison binds himself to pay **Rebecca Addison** 640£; Condition of Obligation: 320£ to be paid on demand not by Bill or Exchange but only by an order on some merchant in England
Witnessed: **Wm. Hutchison, James Haddock,** and **H. Leman**
Proved in open court by testimony of **Mr. Leman** and **John Michell**

- *folio 188* • Obligation (No date)

From: **Richard Harwood** of Ann Arundel County, Gent.

To: **Robert Tyler** of Prince George's County, Gent.

Harwood binds himself to pay Tyler 1,000£; Condition of Obligation is that the determination of a Prince George's County Jury, **Hugh Ryley**, foreman, shall stand free of any problem from Harwood or his heirs; bounds mention *Bowdle's Choice* and *Brazon Thorp Hall*; also **Col. Beall, Hugh Ryley** and **Robert Anderson, Sr.**

Signed: **Richard Harwood**

Witnessed: **Francis Colliar, Samuell Duvall**, and **Thomas Clarke**

- *folio 188a* • Indenture, 15 Jul 1706

From: **Ninian Beall, Sr.** of Prince George's County, Gent.

To: **James Rankin**, planter of the Province of Maryland

For 40£ a 400 acre tract of land called *Beal's Reserve* in Prince George's County on the west side of the Patuxent River and the east side of the main branch of Piscattaway; bounded by *Forrest* surveyed for **Thomas Brooke**

Signed: **Ninian Beall**

Witnessed: **R. Bradly** and **James Stoddart**

Memorandum: 15 Jul 1706 **Ninian Beall, Sr.**, and **Ruth** his wife, acknowledged deed

Alienation: **James Rankin** paid the sum of 16s

- *folio 189* • Indenture, 11 Aug 1707

From: **Clarke Skinner** of Calvert County

To: **Phillip Tottershell** of Prince George's County

For the sum of 30£ a 110 acre part of land called *Ladsford's Guift*; bounded by land belonging to **Barnard Johnson** and land laid out for **Cornelius Caniday** now owned by **Ignatius Craycroft**

Signed: **Clarke Skinner**

Witnessed: **Ric. Marsham** and **James Greenfeild**

Memorandum: 11 Aug 1707 **Ruth Skinner**, wife of Clarke, examined by **Thomas Greenfeild**

Alienation: 24 Sep 1707 **Phillip Tottershell** paid the sum of 4s/5p

- *folio 190* • Indenture, 26 Jun 1707

From: **Richard Lancaster**, merchant of London in the Kingdom of England

To: **Hugh Abrahams**, planter of Prince George's County

For the sum of 200£ a 207 acre tract of land part of a greater tract called *New Castle* being part of the greater tract called *Essington*; bounded by land of **Joseph William**

Signed: **Rich'd Lancaster**

Memorandum: Deed acknowledged by **Richard Lancaster** before **Rob't Tyler** and **Tho. Cleggett**

Alienation: **Hugh Abrahams** paid the sum of 4s/2p

- *folio 191* • Indenture, 26 Aug 1707

From: **Ignatius Craycroft** of Prince George's County, Gent.

To: **Charles Diggs** of Prince George's County

Charles Diggs married **Sophia Craycroft**, the daughter of Ignatius, who died after the marriage but before the marriage portion was paid; Craycroft gives Diggs a tract of land Craycroft bought from **Joseph Letchworth** 14 May 1694 on record in Liber R, folio 214 of Calvert County containing 570 acres which by resurvey found to contain 410 acres now in possession of the said **Charles Diggs**

Signed: **Igna. Craycroft**

Witnessed: **R. Bradly** and **J. Gerrard**

Memorandum: 26 Aug 1707 **Ignatius Craycroft** acknowledged deed

Alienation: 26 Aug 1707 **Charles Diggs** paid the sum of 16s/6p for 410 acres "for the use of the Lord Baltimore by order of Mr. **Charles Carroll**"

- *folio 191a* • Indenture, 26 Aug 1707

From: **Jonathan** and **Elizabeth Prather** of Prince George's County

To: **Col. Henry Darnall** of Prince George's County

For 60£ a 100 acre part of a tract of land taken up in 1672 by **John Bigger, Sr.**, dec'd, called

55

Toogood of 450 acres; bounded by *Croome* owned by **Christopher Rousebyes**, land of **Rob't Ridgley**
Signed: **Jonathan Prater** (mark) and **Elizabeth Prater** (mark)
Witnessed: **Nicholas Sewall, Alex'r Beall,** and **John Smith**
Memorandum: 26 Aug 1707 **Elizabeth Prater** examined by **Ro. Bradly** and **Jo. Gerrard**
Alienation: **Henry Darnall** paid the sum of 4s for 100 acres of land

• *folio 192a* • Deed of Gift, 15 Sep 1707
From: **Elizabeth Marsh**
To: **Geo. Athey, Jr.**
    A black heifer given **George Athey**, son of **George Athey, Senior**
Signed: **Elizabeth Marsh** (mark)
Witnessed: **Ruth Hutchison** and **Han. Blackwin**

• *folio 192a* • Letter of Attorney
From: **Richard Lancaster** of London in the Kingdom of England
To: **John Demall** and **Hugh Abrahams**, planters "in" Patuxent River of Maryland
    Power of Attorney to collect debts in the Province of Maryland
Signed: **Rich'd Lancaster**
Witnessed: **Wotell Hunt, John Anderson** and **Henry Boteler**

• *folio 193* • Indenture, 19 Jun 1707
From: **Thomas Ricketts, Sen'r**, of Anne Arundel County
To: **Richard Lancaster**, merchant of London in the Kingdom of England
    For 100£ a 200 acre tract of land known as *Ryley's Discovery* from a tract laid out for Ricketts
    for 360 acres sold to him by **Hugh Ryley** of Prince George's County; lying in the freshes near the
    Patuxent River; upon condition that Ricketts cannot or does not pay the factors of Lancaster 100£
    within 3 years of the date of indenture
Signed: **Thomas Ricketts**
Witnessed: **John Beckett** (mark) and **Easter Abraham** (mark)

• *folio 193a* • Letter of Attorney, 19 Aug 1706
From: **William Smith**, planter of Prince George's County
To: **John Bradford**
    Power of Attorney to collect debts owed Smith
Signed: **Will'm Smith** (mark)
Witnessed: **Ann Wightt, John Wightt,** and **Tho. Gantt**

• *folio 193a* • Letter of Attorney, 21 Aug 1706
From: **Hannah Smith** of Prince George's County
To: **John Bradford**
    Power of Attorney to sell land on the Eastern Branch of the Potomac River; also lands on the
    north side of Potomac River or elsewhere; to collect all debts owing
Signed: **Hannah Smith**
Witnessed: **Ann Wightt, John Wightt,** and **Tho. Gantt**

Att a Prince George's County Court called and hold att Charles Towne ye 25th day of
November in the sixth yeare of the Reigne of our Sovereigne Lady Ann of the Grace of God
of England, Scottland, France and Ireland Queen Defender of the faith
& by her Majesties Justices thereunto authorized & appointed as VIZ
Present ye Worshipfull   Robert Bradly   Robert Tyler   James Stoddart
Wm. Tanyhill   John Garrard   Frederick Claudius

• *folio 194* • Indenture, 8 Oct 1707
From: **Samuell Pacy**, mariner of the City of London in the Kingdom of England
To: **Thomas Smith** of Calvert County, Gent.
    For 350£ two tracts of land being part of *Brookefeild* in Prince George's County on the west side

of the Patuxent River; *Brookefeild* containing 862 acres sold by **Thomas Brooke, Esq'r** to **Major Nicholas Sewell**; one tract of 443 acres bounded by *Wedge*, near an Indian Fort, by an Indian Path, to land of **Robert Ormes**; the other tract containing 100 acres sold by **Thomas Brooke, Esq'r** to **Samuel Pacy** on 29 Oct 1701 bounded by the land of Sewell and Ormes to Mattapony Creeke, through a marsh to the freshes of the Patuxent River
Signed: **Samuel Pacy**
Witnessed: **R. Bradly, James Stoddart**, and **Josh Cecill**
Memorandum: 8 Oct 1707 **Samuel Pacy** acknowledged deed before **R. Bradly** and **James Stoddart**
Alienation: 26 Nov 1707 **Thomas Smith** paid the sum of 11s for 543 acres
Recorded: 17 Jan 1707/8

Ann by the Grace of God of Great Brittain & att a Court held for her said Majesty ye 27th day of Jan'y 1707 by Her Majesties Justices thereunto authorized & appointed   Present ye Worshipfull
Robert Bradly   Robert Tyler   James Stoddart   John Gerrard   Frederick Claudius

---

• *folio 196* • Vide a Letter of Attorney in folio 193a; memorandum 13 Jan 1707 **Ann Wightt** and **John Wightt** made oath that they saw the Power of Attorney signed before Justices **Jural Coram** and **Tho. Greenfeild**

• *folio 196* • Vide a Letter of Attorney in folio 193a; memorandum 13 Jan 1707 **Ann Wightt** and **John Wightt** made oath that they saw the Power of Attorney signed before Justices **Jurat Coram** and **Tho. Greenfeild** (Ed: Folio 193a had two letters of attorney with the same signers and witnesses)

• *folio 196a* • Indenture, 7 Jan 1707
From: **Col. Thomas Greenfeild** of Prince George's County
To: **Robert Owen**, clerk of Prince George's County
    For the sum of 10,500 pounds of good sound merchantable tobacco and cask, a parcel of land containing 134 acres called *The Gores* in Prince George's County in the freshes on the west side of the Patuxent River; bounded by land formerly belonging to **Major Thomas Brooke** called *Brookefeild*
Signed: **Tho. Greenfeild**
Witnessed: **Frederick Claudius, Thomas Cleggett, Joseph Taylor** and **James Haddock**
Memorandum: 7 Jan 1707 **Martha Greenfeild**, wife of Thomas, examined by **Frederick Claudius** and **Tho. Cleggett**
Alienation: 24 Jan 1707 **Robert Owen** paid 2s/9p for land called *The Gores*

• *folio 197a* • Indenture, 26 Nov 1707
From: **James Moor** of Prince George's County
To: **Benjamin Berry** of Prince George's County
    For 25£ a parcel of land called *Potern Wick* in Prince George's County; bounded by a branch that "issueth out of" St. Charles Branch, by land of **Thomas Cleggett** called *Weston*, by Deep Branch, by land of **William Ludwell**, and by land called **Berry Fortune**; containing 35 acres
Signed: **James Moore**
Witnessed: **Tho. Cleggett** and **Henry Acton**
Memorandum: 26 Nov 1707 **Mary Moore**, wife of James, examined by above witnesses
Alienation: 4 Feb 1707 **Benjamin Berry** paid 1s/6p for 35 acres of *Potern Wick* now called *Berry's Addition*

• *folio 198a* • Indenture, 30 Aug 1707
From: **Nathaniell** and **Susan Magruder** of Prince George's County
To: **Thomas Addison** of Prince George's County, Gent.
    For 51£ a 93 acre part of land called *Bero Plaine* in Prince George's County; beginning at the mouth of St. John's Creek
Signed: **Nathaniell Magruder** (mark) and **Susan Magruder** (mark)
Witnessed: **Thomas Greenfeild, George Jones** and **James Haddock**
Memorandum: 30 Aug 1707 **Susan Magruder** examined by **Tho. Greenfeild**

- *folio 199a* • Indenture, 12 Aug 1707
From: **John Fendall** of Charles County and **Elizabeth** his wife; **Joseph Harrison** of Charles County and **Mary** his wife; **Barbary Ryley** widow of Charles County
To: **Thomas Addison** of Prince George's County, Gent
    For 9,000 pounds of tobacco a 300 acre parcel of land called *Berry* on the east side of the Annocostine (Anacostia) River in Charles County; bounded by land of **Thomas Dent**
Signed: **John Fendall, Elizabeth Fendall** (mark), **Joseph Harrison** (mark), **Mary Harrison** (seal), and **Barbara Ryley** (seal)
Witnessed: **Phillip Lynes, John Countee, William Willkeson** and **James Haddock**
Memorandum: **Elizabeth Fendall, Mary Harrison** and **Barbara Ryley** examined before **Phillip Lynes, John Countee** and **Will'm Wilkeson**
Certification: **John Countee** and **William Willkeson,** Gent. of Charles County acknowledged deed according to an Act of Assembly of this Province before **Edm'd Howard,** Clerk Charles County; Public Seal of Charles County affixed 12 Sep 1707

- *folio 200a* • Indenture, 16 Dec 1707
From: **Robert Brooke,** planter of Calvert County
To: **John Smith** of Hall's Creek, merchant of Calvert County
    Charles, Baron of Baltimore, granted **Baker Brooke, Esq'r** and **Robert Brooke,** Gent, both of Calvert County all that parcel of land called *Brooke Wood* on the south side of the Patuxent River in Prince George's County; inherited by **Baker Brooke, Esq'r** and **Katherine** his wife dated 14 Feb 1694; then to **Robert Brooke;** for 126£/10s 350 acres called *Brooke Wood;* bounded by land of **Roger Brooke** and land of **Baker Brooke**
Signed: **Robert Brooke**
Witnessed: **John Mackall** and **Henry Cox**
Memorandum: 21 Nov 1707 **Grace Brooke** wife of Robert examined by **John Mackall & Henry Cox**
Alienation: 26 Feb 1707 **John Smith** paid the sum of 7s by order of **Charles Carroll**

- *folio 202* • Vide ye conveyance in folio 184; 2? Mar 1707/8 the sum of 12s paid for 300 acres of land called *Ridgly's & Taylor's Chance*

Att a Prince George's County Court held att Charles Towne ye 23d day of March in the Seventh year of ye Reigne of our Sovereigne Lady Ann by ye Grace of God of England, Scottland, France and Ireland Queen Defender of the faith & by her Majesties Justices thereunto authorized and appoynted as VIZ   Present the Worshipfull Robert Bradly Robert Tyler James Stoddart William Tanyhill Frederick Claudius   Commissioners

---

- *folio 202* • Indenture, 13 Mar 1707
From: **Samuel Lyles,** planter of Calvert County and **Ann** his wife
To: **James Bowles,** merchant of St. Mary's County, Gent.
    For 40£ a tract of land called *Cuckholls Delight* in Prince George's County on the north side of the Eastern Branch of the Potomac River formerly laid out for **Thomas Green;** bounded by land of **James Mullikin**
Signed: **Samuel Lyle** (mark)
Witnessed: **Wm. Derumple, Rob't Sollers,** and **Tho. Long**
Memorandum: 13 Mar 1707 sale acknowledged by **Ann Lyles** before **Wm. Holland**

- *folio 202a* • Indenture, 24 Sep 1707
From: **Col. Ninian Beall** of Prince George's County, Gent
To: **John Joyce,** planter of Prince George's County
    For 16,000 pounds of merchantable tobacco a 50 acre tract of land called *Adventure* in Prince George's County; bounded by *Major's Lott,* and land of **James Millikin**
Signed: **Ninian Beall**
Memorandum: 24 Sep 1707 **Ruth Beall** examined by **Rob. Tyler** and **J. Gerrard**
Witnessed: **Rob't Tyler, J. Gerrard** and **Clem't Hill, Jr.**
Alienation: **John Joyce** paid the sum of 2s for the 50 acres of land

- *folio 203a* • Deed of Gift, 15 Jul 1706

From: **Ninian Beall, Sr.** of Prince George's County

To: **Charles Beall**, carpenter of Prince George's County, son of **Ninian Beall, Sr.**

For "natural love and affection" a 440 acre parcel of land called *Batchelor Hope* in Prince George's County on the north side of Oxon Branch; bounded by the land belonging to **Ralph Smith** and the line of *Arran*

Signed: **Ninian Beall**

- *folio 204* • Indenture, 21 Feb 1707

From: **Arther Turner**, planter of Westmoreland County in the Colony of Virginia

To: **Thomas Addison** of Prince George's County, Gent.

For 3,000 pounds of tobacco 400 acres of land called *Batchelor's Harbour* given by the will of the late **Alexander Smith** of Charles County to **Mary Turner**, his daughter and late wife of **Edward Turner**, mother of above **Arther Turner**

Signed: **Arther Turner** (mark)

Witnessed: **Wm. Hutchison** and **Wm. Gardiner**

Memorandum: **Arthur Turner** acknowledged the deed before **Wm. Tannehill** and **Henry Acton**

Alienation: **Thomas Addison** paid the sum of 8s

- *folio 204a* • Indenture, 13 Mar 1707

From: **Edward Battson** of Calvert County, Gent.

To: **Henry Cox** of Calvert County, Gent

By deed of grant from Lord Baltimore 10 Jun 1706 the land called *Battson's Vineyard Rectified* in Prince George's County on the west of the Patuxent River and south-west side of the North Branch of the said River containing 800 acres; mentions *Snowden* and *Manor of Calverton*; **Henry Cox**, son and heir of the late **Henry Cox** of Calvert County the 16 Aug 1707 released to **Nathan Smith** of Calvert County, Gent., a 300 acre tract of land lying at Lyons Creek at the request of **Edward Battson**

Signed: **E. Battson**

Witnessed: **Jo'n Leach** and **James Heigh**

Memorandum: 16 Mar 1707 **Amy Battson**, wife of Edward, examined by above witnesses

Certification: 29 Mar 1708 Calvert County Clerk **Edw'd Botteler** verified **John Leach** and **James Heigh** as Justices of Calvert County

Alienation: **Henry Cox** paid the sum of 1£/12s for the 800 acres

- *folio 206* • Resurvey, 17 Nov 1707

Thomas Hillary, son and executer of the will of **Thomas Hillary**, late of Calvert County requests recording of survey and division of *Three Sisters* in Prince George's County; **John Hillary** receives 400 acres; **Thomas Hillary** receives 240 acres; **Elinor Hillary**, widow, 250 acres now in possession of **Col. Walter Smith**; for **Barruck** and **Thomas Williams** 200 acres also in possession of **Col. Smith**; this patent believed to contain 1,050 acres actually contained 1,090 acres; (see platt of *Three Sisters* on following page)

- *folio 206a* • Letter of Attorney, 31 Oct 1707

From: **Charles Calvert** of Stafford County in Virginia

To: **Thomas Sprigg** of Prince George's County, Gent.

Appointment of "my well beloved cousin" **Thomas Sprigg** as attorney to handle matter of land in Prince George's County sold to "my dear and well beloved brother" **Richard Calvert** of St. Mary's County; deed dated 1701

Signed: **Charles Calvert**

Witnessed: **Thomas Bodband** (mark), **Thomas Luck** (mark), and **Roudoch Bowling** (mark)

Acknowledgement: 1 April **Charles Calvert** acknowledged the document before **Joseph Manning** and **Gerald Fowke**

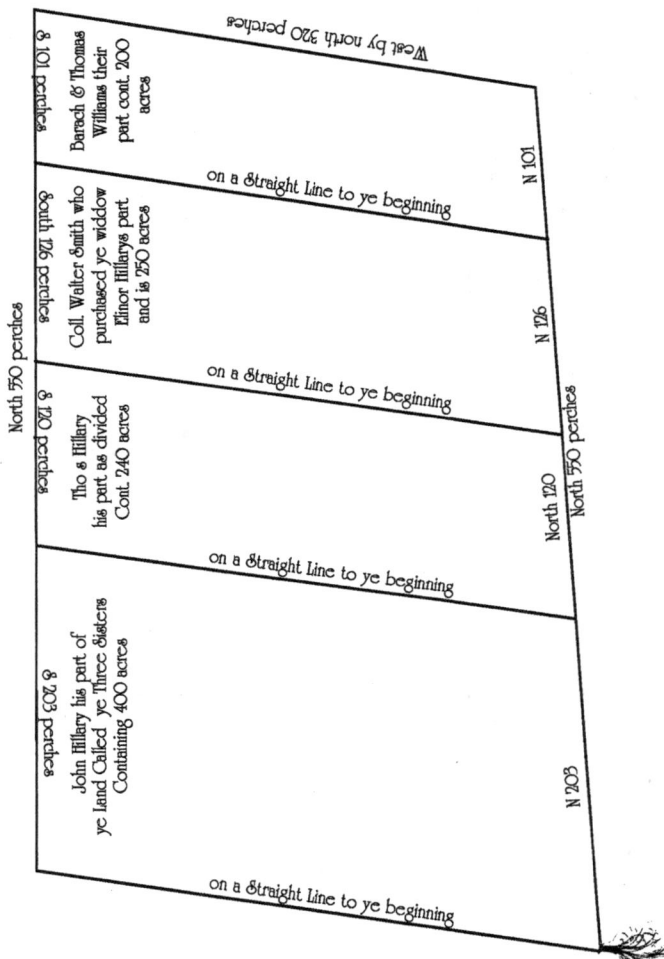

West by north 320 perches

Barrach & Thomas Williams their part cont. 200 acres

8 101 perches

on a Straight Line to ye beginning

N 101

Coll. Walter Smith who purchased ye widdow Elinor Hillarys part and is 250 acres

South 126 perches

on a Straight Line to ye beginning

N 126

North 550 perches

Tho s Hillary his part as divided Cont. 240 acres

8 120 perches

on a Straight Line to ye beginning

North 120

North 550 perches

John Hillary his part of ye land Called ye Three Sisters Containing 400 acres

8 203 perches

on a Straight Line to ye beginning

N 203

This Land called the Three Sisters by pattent is said to be one thousand and fifty acres but upon examination the lines exprest in the pattent conteineing one thousand and ninety acres which gives to each party according to will for Thomas Hillary two hundred and forty acres and is platted by a seale of fifty perches in an inche this 17th day of November 1707

by me   John Brooks

(Unfortunately space did not permit reproducing exact size of this and other plats, so the above measurement is not valid)

- *folio 207* • Indenture, 13 Jul 1701
From: **Charles Calvert** of Charles County, Gent.
To: **Richard Calvert** of St. Mary's County, Gent.
   For 10£ a 600 acre parcel of land on Piscattaway Creek
Signed: **Charles Calvert**
Witnessed: **Robert Bowing** (mark), **Thomas Kuck** (mark) and **Robert King** (mark)
Memorandum: 6 Apr 1708 endorsement; **Thomas Sprigg** examined before **Rob't Tyler** and **Fred'ck Claudius** re Letter of Attorney

- *folio 207a* • Indenture, 31 Jan 1706
From: **John Brown, Sr.,** planter of Prince George's County
To: **Griffeth Jones,** cooper of Prince George's County
   For 7,000 pounds of good tobacco a tract of land called *Warmister* on the east side of Collington Branch in Prince George's County; bounded by land of **Cap. Brock**
Signed: **John Browne**
Witnessed: **John Browne, Jr., Thomas Broome, J. Gerrard,** and **Abraham Clarke**
Memorandum: 31 Jan 1706 **Mary Browne,** wife of John, examined by **Rob't Tyler** and **J. Gerrard**
Alienation: 25 Jun 1707 **Griffeth Jones** paid the sum of 1s/8p

- *folio 208a* • Deed of Gift
From: **John Moberly, Sr.,** of Prince George's County gives the following five sons gifts and their freedom to work for themselves at age 16:
To: **John Moberly** one red cow called Goulde and one sow shoat
To: **James Mobberly** one pied heifer called May, one sow shoat, and one dark colored horse colt
To: **William Moberly** one black heifer called Voluntine, one sow shoat & a dark colored gelding
To: **Edw'd Mobberly** one black 2 year old heifer called Prim and one sow shoat
To: **Thomas Moberly** one black while calf called Hart and on sow shoat

---

Att a Prince George's County Court held att Charles Towne ye 2d day of June for
our Sovereigne Lady Ann by the Grace of God of England, Scottland, France and Ireland
Queene by her Majesties Justices thereunto authorized and appoynted as VIZ

- *folio 209* • Indenture, 11 May 1708
From: **William Conley,** planter of Prince George's County
To: **James Bowles,** merchant of St. Mary's County
   For 122£/12s/8p a 70 acre tract of land called *Gore* in Calvert County now Prince George's County on the west side of Patuxent River and the north side of Brooke Creeke; bounded by *Brookewood, Brookefeild* and Mattapany main run; in the *Manor of Calverton*; another parcel called *Double Goode*; one Negro woman called Moll about 32 years old; 3 cows and calves; payment to be made before 5 Mar 1708/9
Signed: **Wm. Congley**
Memorandum: 11 May 1708 examination of **Ann Congley,** wife of William, examined by **Frederick Claudius** and **Alex'r Magruder**

- *folio 210* • Indenture, 1 Aug 1707
From: **William Austin** and **Ann** his wife of Prince George's County
To: **George Harris,** merchant of Prince George's County
   Ann being the only daughter and heir-at-law of the late **William Rought** of Calvert County; for 43£ a 3 acre parcel of land part of *Twiver* formerly owned by **William Rought;** lying on the west side of the Patuxent River in Prince George's County formerly in Calvert County; bounded by the main swamp of King's Creek, Nottingham Town, **Mr. Bradford's** Lot; formerly sold by **Ann Walker** now wife of **William Austin**
Signed: **William Austin**
Witnessed: **Thomas Greenfeild, Frederick Claudius,** and **Wm. Joseph**
Memorandum: 7 Aug 1707 **William** and **Ann Austin** examined by above witnesses
Alienation: 10 Jul 1708 the sum of 1s/9p paid by **Cap. George Harris**

- *folio 211a* • Indenture, 24 May 1708
From: **William Collins**, planter of Baltimore County
To: **Joshua Cecell** of Prince George's County
"For and in consideration of a competent sum of money" several tracts of land in Prince George's County inherited by **William Collins** from his late grandfather **George Collings** of Calvert County called *Harme, Mansfeild, Collins Comfort* and *Twiver*
Signed: **William Collings** (mark and seal)
Witnessed: **Tho. Greenfeild** and **Cornelius White**
Endorsement: **William Collings** ack'd deed before **Ken. Chesedline** and **Tho. Greenfeild**

- *folio 212* • Gift, 1 Jun 1708
From: **John Mobberly**, planter of Prince George's County
To: **Elizabeth Mobberly**
"Being of good and perfect mind" for "good causes and considerations" gives to his "now wife all goods, chattles, and implements" and any increase in livestock
Signed: **John Mobberly**
Witnessed: **Rich'd Duckett** and **Mary Stone** (mark)

- *folio 213* • Receipt, 7 Aug 1706
Rec'd of **William Wattson** in Patuxent 4 hogshead of tobacco marked and numbered as in ye "margent" and shipped on board ye Preservation, **Thomas Emes**, Commander, at ye rate of 14£ per ton and consigned to **Capt. Richard Beach** in London
Signed: **Dan'll Lambeth** for **Rich'd Beach**

Att a Prince Georges County Court held att Charles Towne ye 2nd day of August in the seventh yeare of the reigne of our Sovereigne Lady Ann by ye Grace of God of Great Britain defender of the the faith by her Majesties Justices thereunto authorized and appoynted
    Present ye Worshipfull   Rob't Bradly   Rob. Tyler   James Stoddart   John Gerrard
                            Frederick Claudius   Henry Acton   Tho. Cleggett   Fra. Marbury

---

- *folio 213a* • Indenture, 24 Jun 1708
From: **Col. Ninian Beall** of Prince George's County, Gent.
To: **Benjamin Wallingford**, planter of Prince George's County
For 39£ a 250 acre tract of land called *Wallingsford's Purchase* being part of a larger tract called *Beall's Pleasure* lying east of the Eastern Branch and the south side of Beaverdam Branch of the Potomac River in Prince George's County
Signed: **Ninian Beall** and **Ruth Beall**
Witnessed: **William Tanyhill** and **Tho. Cleggett**
Endorsement: 22 Jun 1708 **Ninian** and **Ruth Beall** acknowledged deed before above witnesses
Alienation: **Benjamin Willingsford** paid the sum of 10s

- *folio 214a* • Transfer of Title, 7 Nov 1707
Andrew Hambleton transfers of right and title of lot number 58 in the Towne of Marlburrough to **William Offett**
Witnessed: **John Warren**, Clerk of Marlborough

- *folio 215* • Transfer of Title, 10 Mar 1707
Alex'r Dehemossa of Prince George's County sold lot and house number 33 in Towne of Marleburrough for 5,000 pounds of Tobacco to **Christopher Smithers**
Witnessed: **John Warren**, Clerk

- *folio 215* • Royal Appointment, 8 Jan 1705
From: **Philemon Loyd**
To: **Edw'd Willett**, Gent.
Sir Thomas Laurance, Baron, Secretary of Maryland for Queen Ann, appointed **Philemon**

Loyd Deputy Secretary at Large of Maryland; Loyd now appoints **Edward Willett** to be Clerk and Keeper of the Records of Prince George's County Court

- *folio 215* • Transfer of Title, 3 Feb 1707
  James Stoddart sells lot # 43 in Charles Towne to **Christopher Beane** for 1,000 pounds of tobacco
  Signed: **James Stoddart** before **Edward Willett**

- *folio 215* • Transfer of Title, 4 Aug 1708
  For 350 pounds of tobacco accepted 10th of July **Ninian Beall** sells lot number 60 in the town of Marlboro to **Christopher Thompson**
  Signed: **Ninian Beall** before **Clement Hill** and **John Lashly** (mark)

- *folio 216* • Indenture, 24 Aug 1708
  From: **William Sellby**, planter of Prince George's County
  To: **William Rothery**, tailor of Prince George's County
  For 5s and diverse other goods, causes and considerations a 100 acre tract of land in the freshes of the Patuxent River near Mattapony Landing in Prince George's County being part of *Twiver*; mentions **William Selby, Sr.** and **William Downing**
  Signed: **Will. Selby**
  Witnessed: **John Gerrard** and **Alexd'r Magruder**
  Memorandum: **Sarah Selby**, wife of William examined before above witnesses
  Alienation: 28 Sep 1708 **William Rothery** paid the sum of 2s for 100 acres

- *folio 217* • Indenture, 20 Jan 1706
  From: **Murphy Ward**, planter of Prince George's County
  To: **Sam'll & Jno. Ranger** of Prince George's County
  For 8,000 pounds of tobacco 249 acres of land called *Londondary* in Prince George's County on the west side of the Patuxent River of the *Manor of Calverton*
  Signed: **Murphy Ward**
  Witnessed: **Frederick Cladius** and **James Haddock**
  Acknowledgement: 2 Jan 1706 **Mary Ward** wife of Murphy acknowledged deed before **Thomas Greenfield** (Ed: First spelling of "field" where the i is written before the e)
  Payment: **Samuel** and **John Ransher** paid the 8,000 pounds of tobacco
  Alienation: 24 Jan 1707 **Henry Botler** paid the sum of 10s for 250 acres of land

- *folio 219* • Indenture 15 Dec 1707
  From: **Samuell Ranger & John Ranger**, carpenters of Prince George's County
  To: **Henry Botler** of Prince George's County, Gent.
  For 42 £/10s a tract of 249 acres called *London Derry;* bounded by a branch out of *Zakiah*; Royal mines excepted
  Signed: **Sam'll Ranger** (mark) and **Jno. Ranger** (mark)
  Witnessed: **Fredrick Cladius, Alexd'r Magruder** and **Josh. Cecil**
  Memorandum: 15 Dec 1707 **Ann Ranger**, wife of Samuell examined by Cladius and Magruder
  Alienation: **Henry Boteler** paid the sum of 4s

- *folio 221* • Quit Claim Deed, 4 Dec 1707
  From: **Murphy Ward**, son and heir of the late **Murphy Ward** of Prince George's County
  To: **Henry Boteler**
  For 1s all rights to land called *Londonderry*
  Signed: **Murphy Ward**
  Witnessed: **Fredrick Cladius, Alexd'r Magruder** and **Josh. Cecell**

- *folio 222* • Indenture, 8 Jul 1708
  From: **Robert Tyler** of Prince George's County, Gent.
  To: **Richard Duckett**, County Clerk of Anne Arundel County
  For 40£ a 100 acre plantation called *Duckett's Hope*, part of a tract called *Tyler's Discovery* in Prince George's County between land called *Enfield Chase* owned by **John Llewellin** and *Cattail*

Meadows belonging to **Robert Anderson**; bounded by *Ample Grange* owned by **John Boyd** and **Matthew Mackabey's** land
Signed: **Robert Tyler**
Witnessed: **John Gerrard** and **Thomas Clegett**
Memorandum: 8 Jul 1708 **Susannah Tyler**, wife of **Robert** examined by above witnesses
Alienation: **Richard Duckett** paid the sum of 4s for the 100 acres
(Ed: *Amptill Grange* on the Hienton map of Prince George's Co. was written as *Ample Grange* in this document and *Enfield Chase* as *Enfield Chance*)

• *folio 224* • Indenture, 22 Sep 1708
From: **Nicholas Dawson** of Prince George's County, Gent., and **Mary** his wife
To: **William Hutchinson**
For 16£ a 181 acre tract of land in Prince George's County formerly Charles County called *Carrick Fargus* surveyed for **Robert Doyne**, dec'd; descended to his daughters **Sarah Doyne**, **Virlinda Doyne** and **Mary Doyne**, now wife of **Nicholas Dawson**; bounded by *Friendship, Vain,* Kisconcho Creek, *Locust Thickett,* the land of **Randolph Hinson**
Signed: **Nicholas Dawson** and **Mary Dawson**
Witnessed: **Henry Acton, Francis Marbry,** and **Tho's Noble**
Memorandum: 22 Sep 1708 **Nicholas Dawson** and **Mary Dawson** acknowledged sale of all their third part of the within named tract of land before **Francis Marbry** and **Henry Acton**
Alienation: 5 Oct 1708 **William Hutchison** paid the sum of 2s/6p

• *folio 226* • Vide the Deed in folio 178; 7 Oct 1708/9 Rec'd from **William Harbert** the sum of 10s for the land called *Nattingee* of 500 acres from **Phillip Lynes**

• *folio 226* • Pursuant to an Act of Assembly of this Province begun and held at Annapolis 2 Apr 1706 and ended the same month in the Reigne of our Sovereign, Lady Queen Ann:
    18 Jul 1706 **Robert Robertson** of Prince George's County records ownership of a lot in the Towne of Marlbrough according to platt no. 6
Signed: **Jno. Warren**, Clerk

• *folio 226* • Indenture, 13 Jul 1708
From: **Richard Wallis**, planter of Prince George's County
To: **William Wilkinson** of Charles County, Gent.
    For 120£ a 200 acre parcel of land being part of a tract called *Chelsey* in Prince George's County given **Richard Wallis** by the will of **James Williams** dated 14 May 1698
Signed: **Richard Wallis** (mark)
Witnessed: **James Stoddart, John Gerrard,** and **James Haddock**
Acknowledged and paid for; same witnesses

• *folio 228* • Obligation, 13 Jul 1708
    Richard Wallis agrees to pay **William Wilkinson** 240£ if above deed is not valid
Signed: **Richard Wallis** (mark)
Witnessed: **James Stoddart, John Gerrard,** and **James Haddock**
Alienation: **William Willkeson** paid the sum of 8s for 200 acres of land

• *folio 228* • Indenture, 23 Nov 1708
From: **Richard Harison** of Calvert County, Gent.
To: **Benjamin Hall** of Charles County, Gent.
    For 400£ a 250 acre parcel part of land called *Partnership* of 800 acres originally taken up by **John Darnall** and **Nicholas Sewall**
Signed: **Richard Harrison**
Witnessed: **Sam'll Chew, Notley Rozer** and **Luke Gardiner**
Acknowledgement: 23 Nov 1708 **Richard Harrison** acknowledged deed before **Robert Tyler** and **James Stoddart**
Alienation: 23 Nov 1708 **Benjamin Hall** paid the sum of 1£/12s for the within 800 (sic) acres

64

- *folio 230* • Indenture 26 Jun 1708
From: **Murphey Ward** of Prince George's County, son and heir of the late **Murphey Ward**
To: **John Delahunt** of Prince George's County
  For 2,500 pounds of tobacco a 120 acre parcel of land being the westernmost part of a tract called *Woodbridge* on the west side of the Patuxent River; bounded by plantation of **Thomas Hall**
Signed: **Murphey Ward** (mark)
Witnessed: **Thomas Greenfield** and **Robert Owen**
Memorandum: 26 Jun 1708 **Elizabeth Ward**, wife of **Murphey Ward** signed acknowledgement

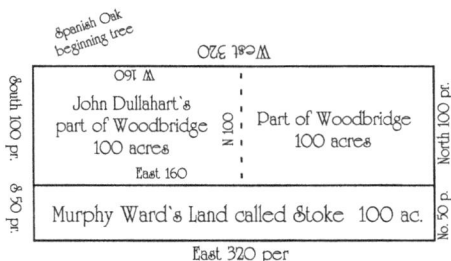

Spanish Oak beginning tree

West 320

W 160

South 100 pr.

John Dullahart's part of Woodbridge 100 acres

North 100

Part of Woodbridge 100 acres

North 100 pr.

East 160

S 50 pr.

Murphy Ward's Land called Stoke 100 ac.

No. 50 p.

East 320 per

- *folio 232* • Ordinance to Regulate Ordinarys, 6 Dec 1708
  As an act of the Assembly regulating Ordinaries will expire at the end of this session, at the suggestion of **Sir Thomas Laurence**, Baron, who had a patent for the Secretary's Office from his late Majesty King William III, commanded His Excellency **John Seymour**, Capt. General & Governor of the province,not to pass any law for the future; the commissioners of the several counties authorized to take security of the several ordinary keepers to keep good rules and order in their houses according to the Law of England; licensing and keeping order to be handled by the county courts
Order of Council Assembly signed by: **Rich'd Bladen**
Read and approved by the House of Delegates, signed by **Rich'd Dallam** and **Ho. Delt**

- *folio 233* •
  Caleb Norris of Prince George's County "hath due to him" 190 acres of land in Prince George's County from **Roger Brooke** of Calvert County, the assignee of **William Williams, Jr.** of said county; being part of a warrant for 200 acres granted Williams 18 Feb 1705; Williams sold 170 acres to Brooke; 179 acres due him from **John Brooke** of Calvert County assignee of **Richard Smith** of same county being part of warrant for 1,742 acres granted Smith 5 Apr 1705; Smith assigned Brooke 300 acres; Condition of Plantations bearing date of 1684; alteration dated 4 Dec 1696; This land called *Cheney*
Henry Darnall, Keeper of Grantor's Seal in Maryland

- *folio 234* • Maryland - Prince George's County
  Pursuant to an Act of Assembly begun and held in the town and port of Annapolis April the 2d 1708 for erecting of town:
  By Virtue of the said act, this day 31 Jan 1708/9 **John Smith, Sr.**, made entry of lot number 42 in the town of Charles Towne; signed: **John Warren**, Clerk

- *folio 234* • Indenture, 8 Jul 1708
From: **Robert Johnson** and **Elizabeth** his wife of Prince George's County
To: **Daniell Thomas** of Prince George's County

To: **Daniell Thomas** of Prince George's County

For the sum of 13£ and 3,000 pounds of tobacco a 200 acre parcel of land in Prince George's County called *Friendship*; bounded by **Robert Middleton** and **Francis Wheeler**

Signed: **Robert Johnson** (mark) and **Elizabeth Johnson** (mark)

Witnessed: **Francis Winson** (mark) and **Jane Ball** (mark)

Memorandum: **Elizabeth Johnson** examined by **Francis Marberry** and **Henry Acton**

Alienation: **Daniell Thomas** paid the sume of 8s for 200 acres

Addendum: 8th month, 25th day, 1704 Warrant granted **Robert Johnson** of Prince George's County for 200 acres of land certified it was surveyed and laid out for Johnson, signed **Luke Gardiner, Jr.,** Deputy Surveyor

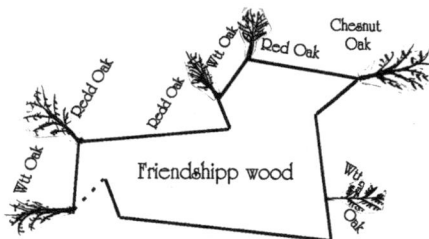

Friendshipp wood

• *folio 237* • Oaths of Allegiance

I A B do sincerely promise and swear that I will be faithful and bear my allegiance to her Sacred Majesty Queen Ann, so help me God

I A B do swear that I do from my heart abhor detest and abjured as impious and heretical this damnable doctrine and position that Princes excommunicated or deprived by the Pope or any authority of the Sea of Rome may be deposed or murdered by their subjects or any other whatsoever and I do declare that no foreign prince persons prelate State of ?Potentage has or ought to have any jurisdiction powers superiority prominence or authority Ecclesiastically or spiritually within the Kingdom of England or the Dominions thereto belonging. So help me God.

The Test: Prince George's County the subscribers do declare that we do believe that there is not any trans___stantiation in the sacrament of the Lord's Supper or the elements of bread and wine at or after the consecration thereof by any persons whatsoever

Oaths listed in their entirety for the following officers of the Crown: Commissioners, Sheriffs, Clerks, Coroners, Envoys, Attorneys and Constables

• *folio 239* • Indenture, 30 Apr 1706

From: **Elizabeth Anderson** wife of the late **Robert Anderson** and **Robert Anderson**, planter, son of the late **Robert Anderson** of Prince George's County

To: **Humphry Beckett**, planter of Prince George's County

For 3,000 pounds of tobacco a 31 acre portion of *First Purchase*, part of a tract of land called *Cattail Meadows*, part of a parcel laid out for **Richard Brogden**; bounded by land laid out for **Robert Tyler**

Signed: **Elizabeth Anderson** (mark) and **Robert Anderson** (mark)

Witnessed: **Robert Tyler** and **Abra. Clarke**

Memorandum: Acknowledgement by **Robert** and **Elizabeth Anderson** and **Jane Anderson**, wife of the younger **Robert Anderson**, examined by above witnesses

Alienation: 22 Jun 1708 **Humphrey Beckett** paid the sum of 1s/3p for 31 acres of land

Letter: 29 Apr 1708 **Jane Anderson** gave consent to above sale in a letter filed with the court

John Talbutt and **William Jervis** mentioned at the beginning of bond **John Anderson** made to **Humphrey Beckett** 8 Sep 1706; witnessed by **Ignatius Mobberly** and **Rich'd Lancaster**

66

Att a Prince Georges County Court held att Charles Towne ye 22d day of Mar 1709 for our Sovereigne Lady Ann by the Grace of God of Great Brittaine, France and Ireland and Queen Defender of ye faith by her Majesties Justices thereunto authorized and appointed

* *folio 243* • Indenture, 18 Mar 1708
From: **William Benson,** planter of Charles County and his wife, **Catherine**
To: **Henry More,** planter of Charles County
    For 6,000 pounds of tobacco a 275 acre tract of land called *Wards Wheele* on the east side of the Piscattaway River; said in the patent to be in Charles Co., but now in Prince George's Co.; bounded by St. Thomas Runn; granted formerly to **John Ward** and last in possession of **William Benson** and **Cathrine** his wife.
Signed: **Will'm Benson** (mark) and **Cathrine Benson** (mark)
Witnessed: **Phill Hoskins, Job. Dodson** and **Jon. Landers**
Acknowledgement: 8 Mar 1708 Charles County acknowledges in Court the alienation by **Edward Howard** of the sum of 7s

* *folio 245* • Indenture, 1 Mar 1708/9
From: **Phillipp Tattersall,** planter of Prince George's County
To: **Tho. Paggett** of Prince George's County
    For 26£ to be paid according to the tenets of the bond already given for the payment of the money and one barrel of Indian corn for a 60 acre parcel of land that did previously belong to **Thomas Paggett** lying near land of **Thomas Hatton,** Gent., and **Joseph Greer**
Signed: **Phillip Tattersall** (mark)
Witnessed: **Tho. Greenfeild** and **Alexd'r Magruder**
Acknowledged: 22 Mar 1708 by **Phillip Tattersall**
Alienation: **Thomas Padgett** paid the sum of 2s

* *folio 246* • Indenture, 1 Jan 1708
From: **Charles Carroll** of Ann Arundel County, Esq'r and **Mary** his wife
To: **Col. Henry Ridgely** of Prince George's County, Gent.
    For 55£ a 100 acre tract of land called *Enfield Chase* originally granted 1 Oct 1683 to **John Lewellin** for 1,600 acres in Prince George's County; bounded by *Cotton* owned by **Henry Land**
Signed: **Charles Carroll** and **Mary Carroll**
Witnessed: **Fitz Redmond** and **Edw'd Carroll**
Alienation: 23 Mar 1709 **Henry Ridgly** paid the sum of 4s
Acknowledgement: 9 Mar 1709 **Charles** and **Mary Carroll** acknowledged deed before **Philemon Loyd**

* *folio 247* • Indenture, 21 Mar 1707
From: **Richard Jones,** planter of Prince George's County and **Ann** his wife
To: **Peter Paggon** and **Isaac Millner,** merchants of London
    For 17,784 pounds of good merchantable leaf tobacco in cask for 100 acres of *Good Luck* lying in Prince George's County on the west side of the Patuxent River
Signed: **Richard Jones** (mark) and **Anne Jones** (mark)
Witnessed: **Tho. Clagett, Tho. Brooke, Jr.,** and **James Haddock**

* *folio 251* • Instructions from Queen Ann to the Justices of Prince George's County 18 Dec 1708 signed **John Leymon**

* *folio 253* • Instructions from Queen Ann to the Justices of Prince George's County 18 Dec 1708 signed **John Leymon**

* *folio 254* • Instructions from Queen Ann to the Justices of Prince George's County 18 Dec 1708 signed **John Leymon**

- *folio 255* • 29 Jan 1706 **Joseph Wilson** paid the sum of 10s and 9 pence for alienation of the 269 acres of land

- *folio 255* • Indenture, 27 9br 1707
From: **Charles Calvert** of Stafford County in Virginia, Gent.
To: **James Neall** of Charles County in Maryland, Gent.
  For 1,000 pound of tobacco a tract of 600 acre part of the 3,000 acre tract of land lying on Piscattaway in Charles County originally granted to **William Calvert**, Esq'r, father of the **Charles Calvert** and the 600 acre part was intended to be given to **Elizabeth Calvert**, daughter of the said William, when she married **James Neale**
Signed: **Charles Calvert**
Witnessed: **Joshua Davis** and **Thom. James** (mark)
Colony of Virginia, Stafford County: Endorsement Nov 1707 signed by **James Westcomt**, Clerk
Memorandum: 15 Apr 1709 Maryland acknowledgement of ownership by **James Neall**; signed **Robert Bradly**
Recorded: 15 Apr 1709

- *folio 256* • Indenture, 31 Mar 1709
From: **Roger Brooke** of Prince George's County, Gent.
To: **John Brooke** of Calvert County
  In consideration of "brotherly love and natural affection" and other causes and considerations a 100 acre portion of *Brooke's Discovery* in Prince George's County patented in the name of **Roger Brooke** and another plat of land called *Hazzard* patented in the name of **Major Will'm Barton**; Barton conveyed to **John Miller** and Miller conveyed to **Roger Brooke** in Prince George's County records; bounded by the main road and one of the original boundaries of *Brooke's Discovery*
Signed: **Roger Brooke**
Witnessed: **James Mackall** and **Mary Parker**
Memorandum before the Justices of Calvert County: **Eliza Brooke** examined by **Will'm Parker** and **Henry Cox**
Certification of **William Parker** and **Henry Cox** signed by **John Warren,** Calvert County Clerk
Alienation: 15 Apr 1709 **John Brooke** paid the sum of 4s
Recorded: 15 Apr 1709

- *folio 258* • Indenture, 31 Mar 1709
From: **Roger Brooke** of Prince George's County, Gent., son of the late **Roger Brooke** of Calvert County, Gent., and heir of the late **James Brooke** of Prince George's County another son of **Roger Brooke**
To: **James Mackall** and **Ann**, his wife, daughter of the late **Roger Brooke**
  The late **Roger Brooke** deeded *Brooke's Reserve* to the late James Brooke 24 Nov 1699 and entered a bond for 500£ that the late **James Brooke** died without issue; thus **Ann Dawkins**, daughter of the late **Roger Brooke** and now wife of **James Mackall** inherited 200 acres called Brooke's Reserve; **James Brooke** had issue which died soon after him; **Roger Brooke** of Prince George's County was brother and heir-at-law of **Roger Brooke** of Calvert County; *Brooke's Reserve* in Prince George's County on the west side of the Patuxent River and the north side of Mattapony Branch contained by late survey 178 acres
Signed: **Roger Brooke**
Witnessed: **John Brooke**, and **Mary Parker** (mark)
Memorandum: 31 Mar 1709 **Elizabeth Brooke**, wife of Roger, examined by **Will'm Parker** and **Henry Cox**
11 Apr 1709 deed acknowledged by the Justices of Calvert County signed by **Henry Warren**, Clerk
Alienation: 20 April 1709 **James Mackall** paid the sum of 7s/3p and a half-pence

Index to Plantations, Plats, and Town Lots

and

Index to People

Index

Plantations, Plats, & Town Lots

Hope Yard, 36
Hope's Addition, 6, 36
Horserace, The, 3
Houp Yard, 10
Houps Addition, 10
Howerton's Range, 9
Hull, 29

Indian Feild, The, 29
Inclosure, The, 21

James Lott, 38
Joseph's Good Luck, 35
Joseph's Park, 46
Joyants Rainge, 49

Kingston, 2
Kingstone, 44

Ladsford's Guift, 55
Lewis Poynt, 46
Limidee, 33
Little Deare, 2, 3
Little Ease, 32, 43
Little Groave, 25
Littleworth, 40
Locust Thickett, 32, 35, 43, 64
Londonderry, 63
Long Looked For, 25
Lundee, 33
Lundey, 31

Major's Lott, 13, 14, 17, 20, 21, 48, 58, 59, 61, 63
Manor of Calverton, 19, 59, 61, 63
Manor of Zechia, 21, 31
Mansfeild, 13, 22, 39, 62
Marlboro Town Lots, 62, 63
Marborrow's Plains, 15
Margery, 1, 2
Margery, The, 20
Marsham's Rest, 15
Marye's Delight, 9
Meadows, The, 6, 17, 30
Mount Calvert Manor, 4, 14, 29, 30, 35
Mount Pleasant, 7, 47, 49
Mullikin's Choice, 14

Nattingee, 51, 64
New Castle, 55
Newfound Land, 21
Newton, 7

Orphant's Loss, 40

Padsworth Farm, 15
Partnership, 36, 64
Pentlin Hills, 49
Perry Hill, 46
Perrywood, 4
Phillip Loudh, 21
Phillip's Addition, 33
Pitchcroft, 4
Plantation, The, 29
Pokemoke, 4
Ponds, 67
Poplar Hills, 28, 46
Potern Wick, 57
Prevention, 28

Quick Sale, 7, 12, 23, 36

Ramsey's Delight, 31
Range, The, 49
Resurvey of Cheroxbury, 22
Revertion, 28
Rich Leavell, 4
Ridgley & Tyler's Chance, 9, 52, 58
Ritch Hill, The, 45
Roper's Chance, 27
Roper's Change, 31
Roper's Range, 25, 26
Rover's Content, 8
Ryley's Discovery, 17, 20, 56
Ryley's Range, 21

Sataraday's Work, 7, 39, 51
Scott's Lott, 22, 34, 35, 42, 43
Shoake, 18
Smith's Green, 18, 26
Smith's Pasture, 18, 26
Snake, 39
Snowden, 59
Something, 20, 27
Spanish Oaks, 14
St. Cullbert Manor, 10
St. Elizabeth, 10, 21, 22
St. John's Value, 16
Stoke, 65
Stoney Plaines, 21
Strife, 31, 52
Swanson's Land, 17
Swaringen, 34
Swaringen's Enlarge- ment, 31

Tannton, 50
Taylor's Coast, 28
Taylor's Marsh, 8

Thomas His Chance, 32
Thomas's Chance, 43
Thompson's Rest, 32, 42
Thorpland, 1, 37, 39, 46
Three Sisters, 59, 60
Thrice Bought, 14
Timberland, 2
Toogood, 56
Tuexbury, 22
Turkey Busard, 6
Twice Bought, 13
Twiver, 49, 61, 62, 63
Twyfoot, 24
Tyler's Discovery, 34, 63

Upper Getting, 34

Vain, 64
Vainall, 49
Vale of Benjamin, 46

Wade's Adventure, 53
Wallingsford's Purchase, 62
Warberton Mannor, 39, 45
Ward's Pasture, 25
Ward's Wheele, 67
Ware, 13
Ware Park, 17
Warmaster, 51
Warmister, 61
Weaver's Purchase, 23
Wedge, The, 23, 33, 57
Western Branch Manor, 11, 12
Westfelia, 46
Westmoreland, 31
Weston, 2, 57
Wheeler's Purchase, 40, 50
White Heaven, 52
Willard's Purchase, 4
Williams Range, 52
Willson's Adventures, 38
Willson's Plaine, 9, 52
Wintersell's Range, 52
Wood's Joy, 33
Woodbridge, 65

Zachia Manor, 31
Zakiah, 63
Zechia Manor, 7, 21

Names have been spelled according to the most common usage in this document.

Hoakloy, Stephen, 38
Hobb, Thomas, 53
  William, 53
Holdsworth, John, 5, 8
Holland, William, 58
Hollaway, John, 36
  William, 36
Hollyday, Thomas, 1, 2, 3, 4, 12, 34
  William, 5, 6
Holmes, Edward, 15, 22, 42
Hope, Walter, 6, 36
Horrey, William, 37
Horton, Margery, 20
  Robert, 20
Hoskins, Phillip, 35, 67
Hoster, Ralph, 20
Hotchill, Thomas, 10
Hourton, Margery, 20
  Robert, 20
Howard, E., 51
  Edm'd, 58
  Edward, 67
Howerton, John, 9
Hunt, Wotell, 56
Hunter, William, 32, 42
  Wotell, 56
Hutchison, John, 19
  Ruth, 52, 56
  Sarah, 10, 19
  William, 1, 3, 5, 6, 7, 8, 10, 12, 13, 14, 16, 17, 19, 20, 21, 22, 29, 31, 34, 35, 36, 39, 45, 48, 49, 50, 51, 54, 59, 64
Hyatt, Charles, 21, 22, 24, 31, 32, 34
  Sarah, 34

Isaac, Richard, 20, 21, 29

Jackson, John, 24
  Joseph, 25
James, Charles, 51
  Elizabeth, 2
  Philip, 3
  Thomas, 2, 3, 68
Jarrell, Richard, 16
Jearell, Richard, 29
Jearoll, Alce, 29
Jervis, William, 34, 66
Johnson, Barnard, 28, 55
  Elizabeth, 13, 65, 66
  Mary, 37
  Robert, 13, 32, 36, 40, 42, 65, 66
  Thomas, 2, 12, 37

Jones, Anne, 67
  Edward, 33
  Elizabeth, 33
  George, 12, 36, 57
  Griffeth, 61
  Johanna, 36
  Richard, 26, 67
  Richard, Jr., 26, 52
  Robert, 22
  Thomas, 46
Joseph, Elizabeth, 35
  William, 35, 46, 61
  William, Jr., 46
Joy, Peter, 2
Joyce, John, 13, 21, 48, 58

Keech, Elizabeth, 39
  James, 39
  James, Jr., 32
Keely, Patrick, 15
Kemp, Thomas, 28
Kernby, Obadyah, 16
Keyfer, Timothy, Capt., 25
King, Robert, 61
Kuck, Thomas, 61

Ladd, Richard, 20
Lambe, John, 11
Lambert, Vincent, 4
Lambeth, Daniel, 62
Lancaster, Richard, 55, 56, 66
Land, Henry, 67
Landers, Jon., 67
Larkin, John, 34
  Margaret, 34
  Thomas, 34, 52
Lashl/e/y, Alce, 27
  John, 1, 27, 32, 63
Laurance, Sir Thomas, 5, 62, 65
Leach, Jo'n, 59
Lecomt, Jno., 28
Lecount, Jn., 28
Lee, Ann, 38
  William, 7, 22, 27, 38
Leman, Hickford, 21, 24, 42, 45, 54
  J., 32
Lemar/r, Ann, 24
  Thomas, 14, 21, 24, 48
  Thomas, Sr., 27
Lenham, John, 32, 42
Letchworth, Joseph, 55
  Thomas, 45, 47
Lewing, Phillip, 32
Lewis, John, 15

Leymon, John, 67
Lingan, George, 25
Linney, William, 36
Linthorne, Elizabeth, 31
  William, 31
L/l/ewellin/g, John, 34, 63, 67
  R., 16
Locker, Thomas, 22
Long, Anthony, 50
  Thomas, 58
Lowe, Henry, 16
Lowry, David, 37, 46, 47
Loyd, Philemon, 62, 63, 67
  Thomas, 6, 18
Lucas, Thomas, 10, 24
Luck, Thomas, 59
Lude, Thomas, 12
Ludwell, William, 57
Lyle, Ann, 36, 58
  Samuell, 36, 58
Lynes, Ann, 50, 51
  Phillip, 50, 51, 58, 64

Mace, Henry, 47
Mackall, Ann, 68
  Benj, 47
  James, 68
  John, 47, 58
Mackebey, Matthew, 17, 20, 21, 34, 48, 64
Macknew, James, 30
  Jeremiah, 30
Macnemarra, Thomas, 46
Magruder, Alexander, 1, 20, 25, 32, 36, 47, 54, 61, 63, 67
  Mr., 38
  Nathaniell, 21, 32, 57
  Samuel, 1, 2, 3, 5, 6, 7, 8, 9, 12, 14, 15, 16, 17, 18, 19, 20, 22, 24, 29, 30, 31, 32, 33, 34
  Susan, 57
Manning, Joseph, 59
Marbury, Francis, 17, 18, 22, 32, 42, 50, 62, 64, 66
Marlbrough, Francis, 47
Marlow, Edward, 30, 31, 32
  Mary, 30, 31
Marsh, Elizabeth, 56
  Gilbert, 53
Marsham, Ann, 15
  Richard, 15, 23, 25, 34, 40, 55
Martin, James, 27
Mason, George, 18, 33

75

Other Heritage Books by Elise Greenup Jourdan:

The Greenup Family
Abstracts of Charles County, Maryland Court and Land Records:
Volume 1: 1658-1666
Volume 2: 1665-1695
Volume 3: 1694-1722
Colonial Records of Southern Maryland:
Trinity Parish & Court Records, Charles County; Christ Church
Parish & Marriage Records, Calvert County; St. Andrew s & All
Faith s Parishes, St. Mary s County

Colonial Settlers of Prince George s County, Maryland

Early Families of Southern Maryland: Volume 1 (Revised) and
Volumes 2-10

Settlers of Colonial Calvert County, Maryland

Settlers of Colonial St. Mary s County, Maryland
The Land Records of Prince George s County, Maryland:
1702-1709
1710-1717
1717-1726
1733-1739
1739-1743

with Francis W. McIntosh

1840 to 1850 Federal Census: Tazewell County, Virginia

1860 Federal Census: Tazewell County, Virginia

1870 Federal Census: Tazewell County, Virginia

9 7 8 1 5 8 5 4 9 1 7 7 3